Books by Beverly Pepper

GLAMOUR MAGAZINE'S AFTER FIVE COOKBOOK

POTLUCK COOKERY

SEE ROME AND EAT

THE
MYRA
BRECKINRIDGE
COOKBOOK

. . . Fay Wray whom I resemble left three-quarter profile if the
key light is no more than five feet high during the close shot.
— *Myra Breckinridge,* CHAPTER 1

THE MYRA BRECKINRIDGE COOKBOOK

BY

Howard Austen and Beverly Pepper

Little, Brown and Company

BOSTON · TORONTO

LIBRARY OF CONGRESS CATALOG CARD NO. 76-99908

FIRST EDITION

*Published simultaneously in Canada
by Little, Brown & Company (Canada) Limited*

PRINTED IN THE UNITED STATES OF AMERICA

For Escoffier, Fannie Farmer

and Gore Vidal

Myra Breckinridge is a dish, and never forget it.
— *Myra Breckinridge*, CHAPTER 2

Anybody who likes sex and food can't be all bad.
— Howard Austen and Beverly Pepper

PREFACE

For as long as I can remember, movies have always "turned me on." It seems only yesterday that there I was, sitting in the dark, being molested, and praying that Lana Turner would crush me in her creamy arms and cover me with hot little kisses, while whispering sensuously in my ear, "Myra, you precious darling, love of my life." Fortunately, this lesbian phase passed quickly. To be precise, it ended on March 21, 1944, to be known always as the day of the "Big O." It was a double feature in every sense of the word. For there on the silver screen was lovable Lon McAllister, breaking my heart in *Home in Indiana*. Even today my hand trembles while writing that name, for the memory of that first moment can never be forgotten. It hit me like the proverbial ton of bricks, my body taut with passion and then . . . Oh, Lon baby, I vowed then and there that if we ever met, I'd really show you what it's like to be home in Indiana. And no matter where you are today that promise still holds true.

The other feature was *Cover Girl* with Rita Hayworth (later to become the Princess Rita, wife of international playboy Ali Khan) and Gene Kelly (a first rate actor-dancer who even today functions as one of Hollywood's working directors) plus all-time favorite Phil Silvers. Before breaking into that spectacular singing, dancing production number of "Make Way for Tomorrow," they had a marvelous oyster-eating scene. Watching them, I cannot tell you what a craving I, too, suddenly had for oysters. I ran home after the matinée, and crying on my mother's lap, pleaded for oysters or seafood. From that day, my goose was cooked; I just had to taste whatever I had just seen at the movies. Indeed, to this day I cannot emerge from a theater without feeling hungry or horny.

Thus began my double profession of film critic and cook. Since then, it's been from the balcony to the kitchen. If there happened to be an exceptionally good double feature, I would be so exhausted I wouldn't know which way to turn. But please don't think I picked up all my things at the movies. As I blossomed into a lovely, voluptuous young thing, my appetite and tastes increased. They became more sophisticated and there were other tricks I picked up along the way. Naturally, I cooked and cooked and cooked. I was now ready for my first dinner party. He was an importer from Brazil whose contribution to the dinner was some newly arrived nuts from the land of the coffee bean. What a glorious dinner it was! We went from soup to nuts. Heady with success I ventured further into unknown territories. *The Good Earth, Abie's Irish Rose, An American in Paris, Andy Hardy* — all produced exquisite menus. Being a good sport, I tried them all — Chinese, French, Jewish, Italian. I became adept at all the variations, a master at bringing out all the hidden qualities. So you see, it was only logical that fate would thrust her hand upon me to produce this book — this food guide to the movies. I have tried to satisfy all tastes, no matter how varied or exotic. A little something for everybody, even if you've never cooked before. Who knows, after reading my book you, too, may turn into a Brillat-Savarin, an Escoffier, an Alice B. Toklas (to a man, all of them now up there in the biggest kitchen of them all) . . . or even a Myra Breckinridge.

But before your dreams of glory get out of hand there are some basic facts you must learn to deal with. Aside from the all-important sense of adventure that one must begin with, certain habits must be got into, certain lessons must be learned. Learning how to buy is the first lesson in learning how to cook, for not even Fannie Farmer can tell you what something will taste like when you get it home. Oh, yes, you can squeeze it, feel it, smell it, but that's only groping in the dark. Until that first tentative taste, not even hearsay can provide the all-important clue as to how it will satisfy your own particular palate. Take it from yours truly, learn to shop around. Some good is to be found in everything. Size, color, shape, even texture should be investigated. Freshness and price should be taken into consideration along with popularity and relevance.

Indeed, I have discovered no irrelevant vegetables, no cut of meat — no matter how low its status — from which cannot be drawn some vestige of aromatic succulence. It is true that in America today, all taste has given way to illusion — the luscious rosy tomato devoid of flavor, the blood-red, beautiful piece of meat that contrives to conceal its origin of genus from us — this is the price we must pay for so-called progress. But there are ways. Just as one creates oneself (I have done so, gloriously, for no man can resist me), one also creates in the kitchen. At the same time, you cannot make a silk purse out of a sow's ear (an analogy not quite appropriate for a cookbook, but relevant neverthe-less). Insist on quality — the key to success. There are no bad cooks, but there are bad ingredients. I do not deny that quantity has a definite attraction for some, even most people, and possibly all fetishists. But isn't it true that something small but tasty is so much more gratifying than something large that you can't do anything with? Haven't we all had that experience! The perfect solution is, of course, the something large that you can do something with. However, it is indeed the lucky recipient who finds it in the local supermarket. Still one somehow doesn't give up the search for perfection, and rather than make do with sloppy seconds we seek, discover, learn; which butcher has the best meat, which stand has the juiciest fruit, what supermarket where you can lay your hands on the freshest, sweetest things just in from the country. It's all there, sitting, waiting to be taken home to be trans-formed into a treat — but it's up to you to turn the trick. So whether you're on Main Street or Broadway, put on your walking shoes, America, and join the ranks of those who care to have the very best. And if you don't find that you're a healthier, happier person, then my name isn't Myra Breckinridge.

W E wish to thank the Centro Sperimentale di Cinematografia and its director, Dr. Leonardo Fioravanti of Rome, Italy, and Mr. John Kobal of London, England, for allowing us to reproduce the photographs used in this book from their excellent and vast collections. We also gratefully acknowledge and thank Marc Rambeau for his aid and assistance and without whom this book couldn't have been done.

CONTENTS

THE IMMORTALS   129

ILLUSTRATIONS

COLLECTORS' ITEMS

MYRA'S FAVORITE DISHES

THE IMMORTALS

POTPOURRI

GOOD ENOUGH TO EAT

BEEFCAKE AND CHEESECAKE

WHAT TO EAT AFTER

W. C. FIELDS MEMORIAL SECTION

NOBODY'S PERFECT

All recipes serve six,
unless otherwise indicated . . .

COLLECTORS' ITEMS

One must be thankful for those strips of celluloid which still endure to remind us that once there were gods and goddesses in our midst . . .

— *Myra Breckinridge,* CHAPTER 9

To sit yourself down in front of the television set and watch the late, late show — from which emerges the only true art form of the twentieth century — is bliss. Absolute bliss! Potato pancake in one hand, breast of chicken in the other and Jean Harlow, Carole Lombard, Gail Patrick on the silver screen — a true feast for tongue and eye. To say I am "hung up" (in this sense, a twentieth-century euphemism for a state of infatuation) is to use the mildest phrase possible for my devotion to the magic, the myth and the reality of the movies. Hung up, no! Dedicated, committed to, in love with. As each familiar figure emerges from the mass of dots that give him form, so each cell of my gray matter at once unfurls, rises, like a cheese soufflé, like Juliet running to her well-known lover's arms. The latest version of this all-time classic, directed by Franco Zeffirelli, although not to be dismissed, must still stand the test of time — how it will work on TV. However, I must admit that neither Leslie Howard's buns nor Miss Norma Shearer's breasts were ever shown to as much advantage as are their juvenile, contemporary counterparts. And by the way, if Leonard Whiting and I ever meet I'll give that kid something to talk about at the milk bar. And that's a promise, Lenny baby!

CHARLIE CHAPLIN

THE GOLD RUSH

Shoestring Spaghetti Dinner

Shoestring Spaghetti
(SPAGHETTI WITH CLAM SAUCE)

Shoe-Tender Sole
(FILETS DE SOLE WITH GRAPES)

Asparagus Salad

Boiled New Potatoes

Crème Brûlée

Parker House Rolls

SHOESTRING SPAGHETTI
(Spaghetti with Clam Sauce)

1 pound spaghettini
6 cloves garlic, crushed
½ cup onion, chopped
6 tablespoons olive oil

1 (1 pound, 13 ounces) can tomatoes
3 (7½ ounces) cans minced clams
1 (6 ounces) can tomato paste
¼ cup parsley, chopped

Sauté garlic and onion in olive oil. Drain tomatoes to remove liquid, and add to garlic mixture in skillet. Drain clams. Put juice in skillet. Add tomato paste and parsley. Cook, stirring occasionally, for about an hour. Just before serving, add minced clams. Meanwhile, cook spaghettini according to directions. Drain. Serve with hot sauce over all.

SHOE-TENDER SOLE
(Filets de Sole with Grapes)

6 sole fillets
Salt and pepper
1 cup Court Bouillon (see page 322)
½ cup dry white wine

1 cup white grapes, peeled and seeded
½ cup cream
2 tablespoons butter

Flatten fillets lightly with spatula, then fold them in half. Season with salt and pepper. Lay side by side in a buttered pan. Pour in Court Bouillon and white wine. Cook gently for 10 minutes, until done. Remove to a heated platter. Garnish with grapes. Keep warm.

Reduce cooking liquid over high heat to one-fourth its original volume. Add cream. Remove from heat. Stir in butter. Check seasoning. Pour sauce over fillets and grapes. Set under broiler to glaze sauce.

ASPARAGUS SALAD

2 pounds cooked fresh asparagus
Boston lettuce hearts, refrigerator cold
Oil and lemon dressing

Do not chill asparagus. Serve at room temperature surrounded with tender hearts of Boston lettuce. Dress with a simple oil and lemon dressing.

CRÈME BRÛLÉE

4 egg yolks
2 cups cream
Pinch salt
1 teaspoon vanilla
½ cup dark brown sugar, sifted

Beat egg yolks until thick and lemon-colored. Heat cream to boiling point. Simmer 1 minute. Stir very slowly into egg yolks. Return to heat. Cook in double boiler top over water. Stir constantly, until just thickened. Add salt and vanilla. Pour into 8-inch shallow ovenproof dish. Cover with aluminum foil. Chill not less than 6 hours; preferably overnight.

Thirty minutes before serving, sprinkle brown sugar ¼ inch deep evenly over surface. Work quickly. Place under broiler 6 inches away from heat — leave oven door open — until sugar melts. Return at once to refrigerator. The sugar should become crusty caramel topping.

CHARLES LAUGHTON

HENRY VIII

Crown Roast of Lamb Dinner

Peas and Shrimp Bisque

Henry VIII Crown Roast of Lamb
Mint Sauce

Celery Amandine

French Peas

Wild Rice and Kumquats

Glazed Onions and Carrots

Mixed Greens

Strawberries Jubilee

PEAS AND SHRIMP BISQUE

2 bacon slices, diced
¼ cup sliced onion
1 pound fresh peas, shelled, or 1 package frozen
1 can frozen condensed cream of shrimp soup, undiluted
    (partially thawed as directed on label)
1 can frozen condensed cream of potato soup, undiluted
    (partially thawed)
2 cups light cream
⅔ cup milk
¼ teaspoon Tabasco
3 tablespoons dry sherry

Slowly sauté bacon in saucepan until crisp. Add onion and peas. Cook, covered, over medium heat 10 minutes, or until peas are just tender. Remove from heat.

Add remaining ingredients. Stir gently until well mixed. Cook, covered, over low heat 20 minutes, or until bisque is heated through. Stir occasionally.

Top each serving with a dash of paprika.

HENRY VIII CROWN ROAST OF LAMB
MINT SAUCE

Entire loin of a spring lamb, prepared for
    16-rib crown roast, ribs outside
2 teaspoons salt
½ teaspoon pepper
12 bacon strips
1 cup savory poultry stuffing mix
1 cup hot water mixed with 4 tablespoons
    melted butter
Broiled mushroom caps

Rub lamb with salt and pepper. Wrap strips of bacon around lower part of the crown. Fill center with stuffing, prepared according to directions on package. Cover filling with bacon strips. Trim ends of bones carefully. Wrap each end in aluminum foil to prevent its burning.

Place roast on rack in very hot oven. Sear for 20 minutes. Reduce heat to moderate. Roast for 1½ hours for rare, 2 hours for well done. Baste frequently with hot water and butter mixture for first half hour, then with pan drippings. Remove aluminum foil when done. Replace with paper frills just before serving. Serve with mint sauce and gravy made from pan drippings; garnish with broiled mushroom caps.

MINT SAUCE

2 tablespoons fresh mint, finely chopped
2 tablespoons sugar
¼ teaspoon salt
¼ cup water
½ cup vinegar
½ cup mint jelly

Dissolve sugar and salt in boiling water. Pour over mint. Cover. Allow mint to steep for 5 minutes. Add vinegar. Mix in mint jelly. Stir well. Allow to stand for several hours or overnight.

CELERY AMANDINE

4 cups young celery stalks, sliced
Salt and pepper
4 tablespoons butter
1 tablespoon chives, finely chopped
1 tablespoon onion, grated
1½ tablespoons flour dissolved in 1 cup light cream
½ cup double-strength chicken bouillon
1 cup almonds, blanched, shredded and toasted

Put celery stalks in saucepan. Season lightly with salt and pepper. Add butter. Cover pan tightly. Cook very slowly until celery is tender. Shake pan frequently to prevent scorching. Uncover pan once during cooking and sprinkle celery with chives and onion. When tender, carefully sprinkle with flour-cream mixture. Stir well. Add chicken bouillon gradually. Cook, stirring constantly, until sauce thickens. Boil 1 minute. Stir in almonds and check seasoning.

FRENCH PEAS

2 tablespoons butter
6 tiny spring onions
5 or 6 leaves lettuce, shredded
½ teaspoon salt
1 tablespoon sugar
3 sprigs parsley
2 cups fresh peas, shelled
½ cup water
1 tablespoon butter
½ teaspoon flour

Put butter in saucepan with onions, lettuce, salt, sugar and parsley. Mix in peas. Add water. Bring to a boil. Cover tightly. Cook rapidly for about 15 minutes, until peas are done. Most of the water should be absorbed. Discard herbs. Remove pan from heat. Cream butter with flour. Add to peas. Return pan to heat. Shake peas around until butter and flour have blended with pea juices. Bring to boil. Remove and serve.

WILD RICE AND KUMQUATS

½ cup butter
2 tablespoons onion, chopped
2 tablespoons chives, chopped
3 tablespoons parsley, chopped
2 cups wild rice, washed and drained
4½ cups chicken broth, boiling
Salt and pepper
12 kumquats, diced
6 kumquats, cut in half

Stir onions, chives and parsley in melted butter over low heat until onions have softened. Mix in rice. Cook, stirring constantly, until rice begins to turn yellow and has absorbed the butter. Stir in chicken broth. Add salt and pepper. Turn mixture into a buttered casserole. Bake, covered, in slow (325°) oven about 1¼ hours — until rice is tender. Fold in diced kumquats. Serve garnished with kumquat halves.

STRAWBERRIES JUBILEE

5 cups strawberries
4 tablespoons sugar
1 cup red wine
¼ cup brandy
1 quart coffee ice cream

Wash, drain, and hull berries. Sprinkle with sugar and set aside. When ready to serve, put strawberries in chafing dish with red wine. Heat. Pour heated brandy over berries. Ignite. Stir gently to keep flame lighted as you spoon strawberries over ice cream.

DR. JEKYLL AND MR. HYDE

French Dinner

Mr. Hyde Blood Pudding

St. Germain Pea Soup

Steak au Poivre

Haricots Verts aux Amandes

Endive, Orange and Onion Salad

Dr. Jekyll's Chocolate Mousse

MR. HYDE BLOOD PUDDING

3 large onions, grated
½ pound raw pork fat
¾ cup pork stock (made with a few bones and a *bouquet garni*)
2 tablespoons lard
2 tablespoons flour
4 cups scalded milk
4 cups pork blood, strained through a fine sieve
Salt and pepper
Pork casings
1 teaspoon powdered allspice
⅛ teaspoon powdered cloves
1 teaspoon parsley, powdered or chopped very fine
¼ cup mushrooms, cooked and finely ground

Combine onions and pork fat with pork stock in a large saucepan. Cover. Boil quickly. Lower heat and simmer very slowly 1 hour. Stir occasionally. Blend lard with flour over low heat. Stir in milk. Stir constantly until bubbling. Boil down to half its original volume, stirring frequently to prevent scorching. Stir in the onion-pork fat mixture. Boil. Lower heat. Simmer gently 15 minutes. Stir constantly.

Remove. Pour pork blood in, *all at once*. Season highly with salt and pepper to taste. Add allspice, cloves and parsley.

Cut pork casings into 6-inch lengths. Rinse thoroughly under running water. Soak in cold water 1 hour. Fill each casing ¾ full with blood sausage mixture. Tie at both ends with string dipped in oil. Drop a few at a time into boiling salted water. Slowly simmer about 25 minutes, uncovered. If any of the sausages rise to surface, prick with pin to release air contained in the casings (otherwise they may burst). Remove sausages with a perforated spoon or skimmer. Store in a cool place.

Or buy them in your favorite imported food shop.

ST. GERMAIN PEA SOUP

3 cans cream of pea soup
2 soup cans chicken broth
1 carrot, thinly sliced
1 onion, thinly sliced
2 lettuce leaves
1 sprig mint

½ teaspoon sugar
3 tablespoons butter
1 soup can sweet cream or milk
Black pepper, freshly ground
Croutons

Blend cream of pea soup, chicken broth, carrot, onion, lettuce leaves, mint and sugar in an electric blender. Cook over boiling water 15 minutes. Add butter and sweet cream or milk. Heat through. Serve with black pepper and croutons.

STEAK AU POIVRE

6 sirloin steaks (individual portions)
Salt
5 tablespoons very coarsely ground pepper
5 tablespoons butter
½ cup cognac
1 cup Brown Sauce (see page 322)

Salt steaks. Pound pepper into both sides of steaks. Sauté in melted butter as desired (rare, medium or well done). Remove to hot serving dish. Add cognac to skillet. Heat and ignite. When flame dies, add Brown Sauce. Bring to boil. Pour over steaks and serve.

HARICOTS VERTS AUX AMANDES

1½ pounds tender young string beans; snap off ends
1 small onion, chopped fine
3 tablespoons butter
Salt and pepper
3 tablespoons slivered almonds, toasted

Cook beans in boiling salted water until *al dente* (cooked but still crisp). Drain. Dry on a cloth or absorbent paper. Sauté onion in 2 tablespoons butter until soft and slightly yellow. Season with salt and pepper. Add beans plus remaining butter. Sauté until butter begins to brown. Add almonds and toss lightly.

DR. JEKYLL'S CHOCOLATE MOUSSE

3 ounces sweet chocolate
1 ounce (1 square) unsweetened
    chocolate
¼ cup coffee
3 egg yolks
½ cup sugar
2 cups whipping cream, whipped
Cocoa

Heat chocolate and coffee in top of double boiler over simmering water until melted and well blended. Beat yolks and sugar. Add chocolate mixture and beat well. Blend whipped cream into chocolate mixture. Put in a 2-quart mold and place in freezer or refrigerator to harden. Serve with more whipped cream sprinkled with cocoa.

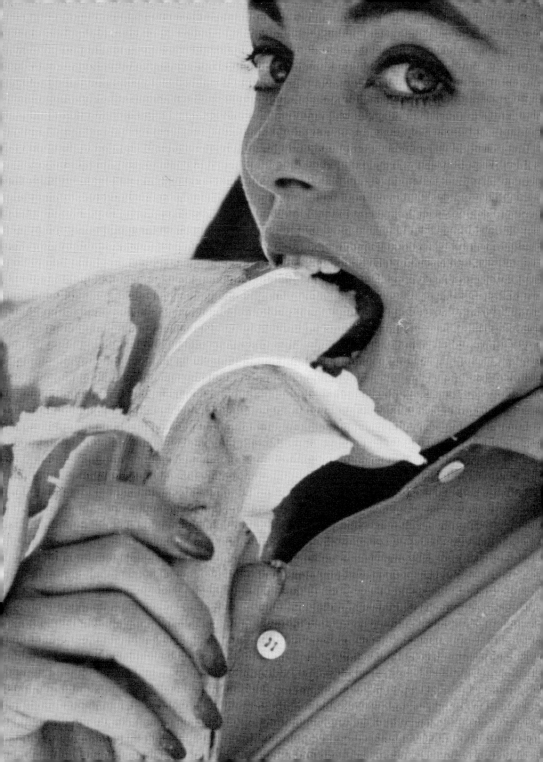

HUGH GRIFFITH

TOM JONES

English Dinner

Bearded Oysters (see page 122)

Roast Prime Ribs of Beef

Horseradish Sauce

Herbed Yorkshire Pudding

Peas and Whipped Mashed Potatoes

Deviled Broiled Tomatoes

Mimosa Salad

Cheese Board

Syllabub

Fruitcake

ROAST PRIME RIBS OF BEEF
HORSERADISH SAUCE

**4-rib roast made of first ribs: close-grained meat
streaked with veins of fat
Salt and pepper**

Wipe meat with damp cloth. Season with salt and pepper. Place fat side up in open roasting pan with no water. Cook, uncovered, in a moderately slow oven, 325°, 18 to 20 minutes to the pound for rare; 22 to 25 minutes for medium, and up to 35 minutes for well done.

If the beef is chilled or frozen, it takes longer to cook.

HORSERADISH SAUCE

**¼ cup drained prepared horseradish
½ teaspoon salt
1 cup sour cream**

Combine horseradish, salt and sour cream. Serve in a small bowl.

HERBED YORKSHIRE PUDDING

**Beef drippings
3 eggs
1¼ cups milk
1 cup flour, sifted
1 teaspoon salt
1 tablespoon parsley, minced
¼ teaspoon each rosemary and thyme**

Heat oven to hot (450°). Pour 1¼ tablespoons hot drippings from beef into each section of muffin or popover pans. Beat eggs until fluffy. Mix flour, salt, parsley, rosemary and thyme with eggs. Mix just enough to make smooth. Pour into pans. Bake 15 minutes. Reduce heat to moderate (350°) and bake another 10 to 15 minutes, or until puffy and brown.

PEAS AND WHIPPED MASHED POTATOES

3 cups mashed potatoes
Salt and pepper to taste
½ cup heavy cream
⅓ cup grated cheese
Cooked fresh peas

Season potatoes with salt and pepper. Pile into buttered baking dish. Whip cream until stiff and spread over mashed potatoes. Sprinkle grated cheese over all. Bake in preheated oven at 450° until cheese melts and browns slightly. Serve surrounded by cooked fresh peas dotted generously with butter.

DEVILED BROILED TOMATOES

6 medium-sized tomatoes
Salt and pepper
Few grains cayenne
Bread crumbs
Butter
1 hard-cooked egg, finely mashed
3 tablespoons butter
¾ teaspoon prepared mustard
3 drops Tabasco sauce
1 tablespoon Worcestershire sauce
1 teaspoon sugar
2 tablespoons wine vinegar
1 large egg, slightly beaten

Cut tomatoes in half. Sprinkle each half with salt, pepper and a few grains of cayenne. Top with bread crumbs. Dot with bits of butter. Arrange on rack of broiling pan. Then: add butter, mustard, salt, a few grains of pepper, 3 drops of Tabasco sauce, Worcestershire sauce, sugar and wine vinegar to mashed egg. Mix thoroughly. Stir in raw egg. Cook over hot water, stirring constantly, 3 to 4 minutes until the mixture thickens. Remove from heat and keep warm. Set aside while tomatoes broil.

Cook tomato halves under broiler until crumbs brown and tomatoes wrinkle. Arrange on heated platter and top each half with a dollop of the sauce.

MIMOSA SALAD

¼ cup olive oil
1 tablespoon lemon juice
½ teaspoon salt
Dash pepper
1 clove garlic, crushed
2 quarts cold crisp mixed salad greens
2 hard-cooked eggs, finely chopped

Combine oil, lemon juice, salt, pepper and garlic in a jar with a tight lid. Shake vigorously. Arrange greens in a salad bowl. Add dressing. Toss well. Sprinkle with chopped egg.

SYLLABUB

(Lemon Cream with Sherry and Brandy)

Syllabub should be served in a tall narrow glass tapering toward the bottom and holding about ½ cup of liquid.

2 lemons
1 bottle dry sherry
2 tablespoons brandy
1 pint cream
1 egg white
2 tablespoons sugar

Peel lemons very thinly and put rind (which must be quite free of bitter white part) to soak in sherry for at least 12 hours. Then take out lemon peel. Add brandy, cream, egg white, sugar and freshly squeezed lemon juice. Whip mixture until cream becomes fairly frothy. Pour into syllabub glasses. Refrigerate at least 6 hours before serving.

ENGLISH FRUITCAKE

(Makes 4 2½-pound cakes or 1 10-pound cake)

1 pound butter
1 pound brown sugar
10 eggs, well beaten
1 pound plumped raisins
½ pound glazed pineapple
½ pound glazed cherries
1 pound seeded raisins
½ pound citron, diced
½ pound orange peel
½ pound dates, pitted and sliced
½ pound fruitcake mix
Grated rind of 1 lemon

½ pound pecans
1 pint brandy
1 cup honey, strained
1 cup dark molasses
½ cup cider
1 teaspoon salt
1 pound flour
1 teaspoon double-action baking
   powder
½ teaspoon each cloves, mace
   and cinnamon

Gradually cream butter with sugar. Add well-beaten eggs. Add fruit and rest of ingredients.

Sift flour; measure. Add baking powder and spices. Sift three times. Add flour mixture gradually. Line 4 2½-pound-size cake tins with greased waxed paper. Bake in 300° oven for 3 hours.

AYLLENE GIBBONS

THE LOVED ONE

Christmas Dinner

Green Soup

Roast Suckling Pig

Asparagus Hollandaise

Chestnut Purée

Flaming Sweet Potatoes

Orange and Avocado Salad

Pecan Pie

GREEN SOUP

6 cups beef stock
3 slices cooked ham, diced
1½ cups raw spinach, minced
½ cup green onion, minced
½ cup raw mixed greens (kale, sorrel and beet tops), chopped

Parsley, tarragon, chives and rosemary, chopped fine
2 tablespoons flour
6 tablespoons sour cream
6 hard-boiled eggs, sliced

If you've an electric blender, put greens together and chop coarsely ½ minute. Boil ham in stock 5 minutes. Add spinach, onion, raw mixed greens and herbs. Simmer slowly 1 hour. Remove pan from heat. Mix flour and enough of the sour cream to make a smooth paste. Stir into stock. Return to heat. Stir until thickened. Add remaining sour cream. Garnish with hard-boiled egg slices in each plate.

ROAST SUCKLING PIG

Suckling pig, about 10 pounds
½ cup celery, chopped
¼ cup onion, chopped
1 clove garlic
3 tablespoons butter
2 cups apples, peeled, cored and coarsely chopped
1 cup mushrooms, sliced
¼ teaspoon thyme

½ cup parsley, chopped
Salt
Apple juice to moisten
1 cup apple juice, boiling
Apple
Cherries
Laurel wreath
Greens

Sauté celery, onion and garlic in butter. Mix with apples, mushrooms, thyme, parsley, salt and enough apple juice to moisten. Stuff pig. Sew or skewer cavity closed. Place a piece of wood in pig's mouth to prop open. Cover ears and tail with foil to prevent burning. Tie legs in place. Roast in moderate (325°) oven 3 to 4 hours, basting frequently every hour. Prick skin in several places to let fat run out. Add apple juice after first hour. Turn once. To serve, remove wood and insert apple. Decorate, using cherries for eyes and laurel wreath around neck. Serve on a bed of greens.

ASPARAGUS HOLLANDAISE

36 asparagus, tied in bundles of six

Snap off tough ends. Cook upright in boiling water in an asparagus boiler — until tender, about 15 minutes. If you haven't an asparagus boiler stand the bundles on end in the bottom of a double boiler. Use top pan inverted as a cover.

Serve with hollandaise sauce.

HOLLANDAISE SAUCE

½ cup butter	Pinch white pepper
4 egg yolks	Pinch salt
2 teaspoons lemon juice	

Put egg yolks and 3 tablespoons butter in top of a double boiler over simmering water. Stir constantly until butter is melted. Add 3 tablespoons butter. As mixture thickens and butter melts, add remaining butter. Continue stirring constantly until butter is thoroughly mixed. Water in bottom pan should simmer slowly, *not boil.*

Remove saucepan from heat. Beat sauce for another 3 minutes. Remove top of double boiler. Add lemon juice, salt and pepper. Replace top of double boiler over hot, not boiling, water. Beat sauce another few minutes.

Should mixture curdle, beat in immediately 1 to 2 tablespoons boiling water to rebind the emulsion.

CHESTNUT PURÉE

2 pounds chestnuts
2–3 cups milk
3 small pieces white celery
Salt and pepper
2 tablespoons butter
3 tablespoons sherry

Cut a gash on flat side of chestnuts and put in very hot oven or under broiler flame for 5 to 6 minutes. Take from oven and remove shells and skins with sharp knife. Cook chestnuts until tender in boiling milk with celery. Drain. Reserve liquid and discard celery. Rub chestnuts through fine sieve or put into electric blender. Season with salt and pepper. Beat in butter and a little of the strained milk used for cooking chestnuts. Add sherry.

FLAMING SWEET POTATOES

6 medium-size sweet potatoes
¼ cup sweet butter
½ cup brown sugar
About 3 tablespoons melted butter
½ cup white rum
1 or 2 lumps sugar

Boil unpeeled potatoes until tender. Drain. Cool. Peel. Cut into ½-inch slices. Brown on both sides in 2 tablespoons butter. Sprinkle with brown sugar. Pour over them remaining butter — melted. Mix well, being careful not to break. Heat rum in large ladle with sugar. Ignite. Pour aflame over potatoes. Toss gently and baste constantly until flame is extinguished.

ORANGE AND AVOCADO SALAD

6 large seedless oranges, peeled and sliced
Peel of one orange
Lettuce
3 small ripe avocados, peeled
Juice of 2 large limes
3 tablespoons Dijon-style mustard
1½ cups mayonnaise
Salt
Parsley sprigs

Place peel of 1 orange in saucepan with cold water to cover. Simmer until soft. Drain. Remove loosened white pith from peel. Shred remaining skin.

Cut oranges into crosswise slices, keeping slices together. Arrange each orange on lettuce-lined salad plate so that it resembles a whole orange. Top with avocado dressing: mash avocados with lime juice, mustard, salt and mayonnaise. Sprinkle salad with shredded orange peel. Garnish with parsley sprigs.

PECAN PIE

Pastry mix for 9-inch pie shell
1 cup pecans, halved
1 tablespoon melted butter
1 cup light corn syrup
½ teaspoon lemon rind, grated
¼ teaspoon powdered cinnamon

¼ teaspoon powdered cloves
3 eggs, well beaten
1 cup sugar
1 tablespoon flour
2 cups whipped cream

Prepare mix as directed on package. Then: line pie plate with pastry. Flute edges. Arrange pecans in bottom of shell. Mix butter, corn syrup, lemon rind, cinnamon and cloves into beaten eggs. Stir well. Blend sugar and flour. Add to egg mixture. Pour over nuts. Let stand until nuts come to surface. Bake in 350° oven for about 40 minutes or until filling is firm and pecans glazed. Serve hot or cold with whipped cream.

RAY MILLAND, CASS DALEY AND WILLIAM HOLDEN

VARIETY GIRL

Deep South Dinner

Asparagus Soufflé

Baked Sugar-Cured Ham

Hopping John

Sweet Potato Pie

Spoon Bread

Green Salad

Deep Dish Apple Pie with Almonds

ASPARAGUS SOUFFLÉ

1 bunch asparagus	4 egg whites, stiffly beaten
1 cup milk	Paprika
4 thin slices onion	Nutmeg
1 bay leaf	Salt
1 clove	White pepper
⅓ cup butter	4 tablespoons Parmesan
3 tablespoons flour	cheese, grated
3 egg yolks	

Trim asparagus, removing all tough ends down to 3½ to 4 inches of the tips. Boil in salted water 15 minutes. Drain. Arrange carefully in a generously buttered baking dish. Scald milk with onion, bay leaf and clove. Strain. Melt butter and blend in flour until quite smooth. Do not brown. Stir in scalded milk. Simmer, stirring constantly until mixture thickens. Remove from heat and cool slightly. Add, slowly, well-beaten egg yolks, seasoned with a little salt, a little white pepper and a dash each of paprika and nutmeg. Fold in Parmesan cheese alternately with stiffly beaten egg whites. Pour over asparagus and bake in moderate (350–375°) oven about 35 to 40 minutes until well puffed and brown. Serve at once.

BAKED SUGAR-CURED HAM

1 tenderized ham	1 cup pineapple juice
30 to 40 cloves	2 cups pineapple chunks
1 egg, beaten	½ pound brown sugar
1 cup domestic champagne	

Remove excess fat from ham. Cook as directed on package. Then score with cooky cutter or knife, making squares. Brush with beaten egg. In each square place a clove. Cover with brown sugar. Set in roaster. Add champagne, pineapple juice and pineapple. Bake 1 hour at 350°, basting every 20 minutes to glaze ham evenly. If liquid reduces too fast during baking, keep adding champagne. When ham is cooked, liquid should be reduced to heavy syrup. Garnish with glazed pineapple chunks.

HOPPING JOHN

1 pound black-eyed peas	8 peppercorns
¾ pound cubed, parboiled salt pork or fat bacon	1 cup washed rice
	2½ quarts boiling water
½ teaspoon salt	Salt
1 large bay leaf	White pepper
1 medium-sized onion	1 large can Italian peeled tomatoes

Wash and pick over peas. Cover with 2 inches cold water. Add pork, salt, bay leaf, onion and peppercorns, freshly ground. Cook till beans are tender. Add more boiling water if necessary. Meanwhile, slowly add rice to boiling water. Cook until tender. Drain. Rinse under hot water faucet. Season with salt and pepper. While rice is cooking, heat tomatoes with 1 teaspoon basil.

Serve rice and black-eyed peas separately; pour peas over a mound of rice, and surround with tomatoes.

SWEET POTATO PIE

½ box prepared pie mix	⅛ cup milk
¾ cup butter	¾ teaspoon ground ginger
¾ cup sugar	2 tablespoons grated orange rind
1½ cups sweet potatoes, grated	

Line an unbuttered 9-inch pie plate with prepared pie mix. Place pie plate in refrigerator while preparing filling. Preheat oven to 300°.

Cream butter. Add sugar. Continue creaming until light and fluffy. Gradually add sweet potatoes and milk alternately. Mix thoroughly. Add ginger and orange rind. Mix again. Pour into prepared pie plate. Bake in 300° oven for 45 minutes, until delicately browned. Serve piping hot with whipped cream on the side.

SPOON BREAD

1 teaspoon salt
2 cups milk, scalded
1 cup corn meal
2½ teaspoons baking powder
2 egg yolks, well beaten
2 egg whites, stiffly beaten

Add salt to milk. Gradually stir in corn meal. Cook in top of double boiler over hot water until thick and smooth. Cool to lukewarm. Add baking powder to beaten egg yolks. Combine with corn meal mush and mix well. Beat egg whites until stiff and fold in. Pour into well-buttered 9-inch square baking pan. Bake in moderate (375°) oven 35 minutes. Serve with a spoon.

DEEP DISH APPLE PIE WITH ALMONDS

About 8 apples, sliced
1 cup toasted almonds, chopped
½ cup melted butter
2 tablespoons tapioca
½ to 1 cup sugar
2 tablespoons rum
1 box rich pastry mix
Thick sweet or sour cream

Fill deep baking dish with the apples. Mix together almonds, melted butter, tapioca and sugar (from ½ to 1 cup depending on taste). Add rum. Pour mixture over the apples. Top with rich pastry, pressing edges firmly to side of baking dish.

Bake in very hot (450°) oven 10 minutes. Reduce heat to moderate (350°) and bake 30 to 40 minutes longer or until pastry is nicely browned. Serve warm with whipped cream.

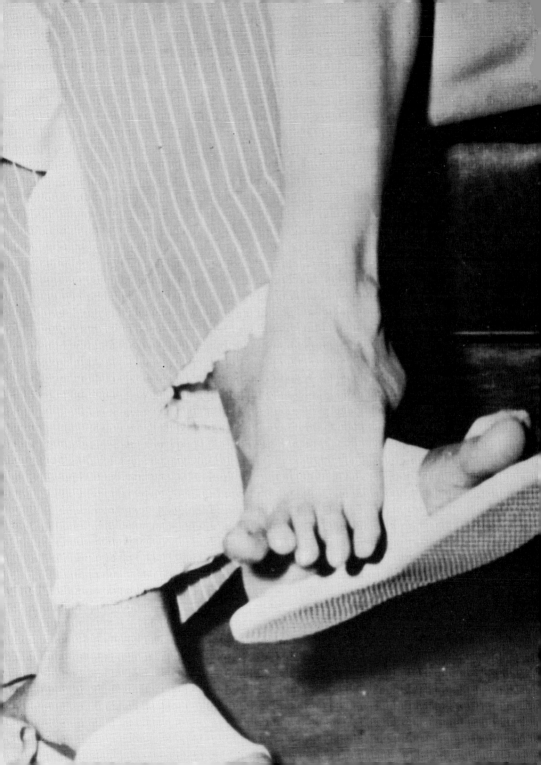

PUBLIC ENEMY

New Orleans Dinner

Mae Clarke Boula Bouillon

Shrimp Rémoulade

New Orleans Chicken Gumbo

Red Onion Salad

Camembert and Crackers

James Cagney Grapefruit Mousse

MAE CLARKE AND JAMES CAGNEY

MAE CLARKE BOULA BOUILLON

3 cups frozen green peas, cooked
3 cups canned green turtle soup
2 tablespoons butter

Salt and pepper to taste
1½ cups sherry
1 cup whipped cream, unsweetened

Blend cooked peas in an electric blender with ½ cup turtle soup until well puréed.

Place in saucepan with butter, salt, pepper and remaining turtle soup. Mix and blend well. Add sherry. Heat to boiling point.

Pour soup in heatproof serving cups. Garnish with whipped cream. Place under broiler to brown the topping. Serve at once.

SHRIMP RÉMOULADE

3 pounds cooked shrimp
1 cup mayonnaise
2 hard-cooked eggs, finely chopped
6 stuffed olives, chopped
1 tablespoon green pepper, chopped
1 garlic clove, crushed

1 tablespoon anchovy paste
1 teaspoon Worcestershire
1 teaspoon dry mustard
Salt
Freshly ground black pepper

Chill shrimp at least 1 hour. Mix remaining ingredients thoroughly to make sauce. Add shrimp. Mix again. Chill again for an hour.

NEW ORLEANS CHICKEN GUMBO

1 (4-pound) roasting chicken, quartered
2 pounds cooked ham cut into 1-inch cubes
2 cups water
2 cups onion, chopped
2 cloves garlic, crushed
2 teaspoons salt
½ teaspoon basil
½ teaspoon oregano

⅛ teaspoon pepper
3 drops Tabasco sauce
Dash cayenne pepper
6 slices bacon
4 tablespoons flour
1 can tomatoes
¼ cup tomato paste
2 teaspoons gumbo filé powder
Rice

Put chicken, ham and onion in water in a deep, heavy kettle. Season with garlic, salt, basil, oregano, pepper, Tabasco sauce and cayenne.

Cover. Simmer until chicken is tender — about 1 hour. Remove meat from broth. Fry bacon until crisp. Drain on paper. Stir flour in bacon drippings until golden. Add to broth with tomatoes and tomato paste. Stir until thickened. Remove chicken from bones. Leave in large pieces. Add the ham to sauce. Add chicken pieces. Cover. Simmer gently 45 minutes. Stir occasionally to prevent sticking. Add crumbled bacon. Stir in filé powder. Bring to a boil. Serve at once with rice.

NOTE: Never reheat gumbo, after filé powder has been added.

RED ONION SALAD

4 red onions, peeled and sliced paper-thin
2 teaspoons salt
Ice water
Ice cubes
½ cup olive oil
3 tablespoons wine vinegar
Anchovy fillets
Black olives, pitted
Pimiento

Sprinkle sliced onions with salt. Cover with ice water and ice cubes for 30 minutes. Drain and dry well. Arrange in layers in a salad bowl. Sprinkle each layer with a mixture of olive oil and wine vinegar. Garnish with anchovy fillets and black olives, and pimiento.

JAMES CAGNEY GRAPEFRUIT MOUSSE

1 tablespoon gelatin
2 tablespoons water
6 tablespoons grapefruit juice
3 eggs, separated
⅔ cup sugar
Grated rind of 1 grapefruit
Raspberry and currant jelly sauce

Soften gelatin in water. Add grapefruit juice. Stir mixture over hot water until gelatin dissolves. Beat egg yolks until they are very light and airy. Add ⅓ cup sugar and the gelatin mixture. Beat egg whites until stiff. Add gradually ⅓ cup sugar and grapefruit rind. Fold into the yolk mixture. Chill in a serving bowl until firm. Serve with raspberry and currant jelly sauce.

REGINALD OWEN, PAULETTE GODDARD AND JUDITH ANDERSON

DIARY OF
A CHAMBERMAID

Maid's Night Out Dinner

Avocado and Crab Meat Cocktail

Lamb Chop Casserole

Corn on the Cob

Dilled Carrots

Watercress and Orange Salad

Peach Cobbler

AVOCADO AND CRAB MEAT COCKTAIL

2 small ripe avocados, peeled
½ teaspoon onion, grated
2 teaspoons lemon juice
¼ teaspoon salt
Tabasco sauce
¾ cup tomato catsup
2 tablespoons chili sauce

1 tablespoon prepared horseradish
½ teaspoon Worcestershire
¼ teaspoon sugar
Lettuce leaves
1 7-ounce can crab meat chunks or
  ½ pound fresh crab meat

Mash half of one avocado. Mix with grated onion, 1 teaspoon lemon juice, salt and Tabasco. Cool in refrigerator. Mix catsup, chili sauce, horseradish, Worcestershire, sugar and 1 teaspoon lemon juice. Chill. Line cocktail glasses with lettuce leaves. Cut second avocado in ½-inch cubes. Mix avocado cubes and crab meat and arrange in cocktail glasses. Serve cocktail sauce over crab meat mixture. Top with remaining avocado half, sliced.

LAMB CHOP CASSEROLE

6 lamb chops, about 5 ounces each,
  cut from leg
2 tablespoons olive oil
2 tablespoons butter
¼ cup raw, lean, chopped ham
1 medium-size onion, chopped
4 medium-size tomatoes, peeled and
  chopped

⅛ teaspoon nutmeg
⅛ teaspoon mace
⅛ teaspoon thyme
⅛ teaspoon allspice
Salt
Pepper

Brown lamb chops in olive oil and butter. When well browned, turn into earthenware casserole. Cook chopped ham in fat left in pan. Add onion over low heat. Stir frequently until mixture just begins to take on color. Stir in tomatoes. Season highly with salt, pepper, nutmeg, mace, thyme and allspice. Cook over low heat 10 minutes. Stir occasionally. Pour sauce over chops. Cover tightly. Bake in moderate (375°) oven 35 minutes. Serve with buttered noodles.

DILLED CARROTS

2 pounds young carrots, cut in thick matchsticks
1½ cups dill pickle juice
3 tablespoons fresh dill, minced
1½ tablespoons chives, minced
1½ cups sour cream

Simmer carrots, covered, in dill pickle juice until tender but still firm — about 6 to 8 minutes. Cool. Chill overnight in pickle juice. Drain. Sprinkle with dill and chives. Garnish with sour cream.

WATERCRESS AND ORANGE SALAD

Fill a salad bowl with alternate layers of thinly sliced oranges, paper-thin onion slices (optional) and crisp watercress leaves. Sprinkle with French dressing (see page 323). Chill thoroughly.

PEACH COBBLER

1 egg
1 cup sugar
1 teaspoon lemon rind
1 teaspoon vanilla
1 cup flour sifted with ½ teaspoon salt and 1 teaspoon baking powder

¼ cup milk
¼ cup butter, melted
3 packages frozen peaches
1 tablespoon lemon juice
1 teaspoon cinnamon
1 cup sour cream
Dash of nutmeg

Mix egg and ½ cup sugar thoroughly. Add lemon rind and vanilla. Add sifted flour mixture. Stir in milk. Stir in butter. Pour into greased, floured 9-inch layer cake pan. Spread smooth. Drain defrosted peaches thoroughly. Sprinkle with lemon juice. Arrange peaches on top of batter. Top with remaining sugar. Sprinkle with cinnamon. Bake in moderate (350°) oven 70 minutes — until cobbler is golden brown and pulls away from the edges of the pan. Cool in pan. Serve warm topped with sour cream garnished with nutmeg.

SPAWN OF THE NORTH

Jewish Dinner

Matzo Ball Soup

Gefüllte Fish

Chopped Liver

Stuffed Cabbage

Cole Slaw

Potato Latkes

Cheese Blintzes with Sour Cream

MATZO BALL SOUP

4 egg whites, beaten stiff
4 egg yolks
1 cup matzo meal
¼ teaspoon salt

1 tablespoon water
Salted boiling water
6 to 8 cups chicken soup

Mix egg yolks with salt and 1 tablespoon water. Stir in matzo meal. Mix in egg whites. Mixture should resemble heavy sour cream. Roll into walnut-sized balls. Drop into large pot of salted boiling water. Cook covered about ½ hour. Remove carefully with spatula. Serve in chicken soup.

GEFÜLLTE FISH

6 ounces fillet of halibut
6 ounces sea bass
6 ounces fillet of carp
6 ounces whitefish
1 medium-sized onion, chopped
3 pieces tender celery, chopped
3 cloves garlic, chopped
¼ teaspoon marjoram
¼ teaspoon thyme

Salt and pepper
2 eggs, well beaten
4 tablespoons parsley, finely chopped
2 cups matzo meal
2 cups cream
2 carrots, sliced
3 lemons, peeled and sliced
2 quarts fish stock

Cut fish in small pieces. Add onion, celery, garlic, marjoram, thyme, salt and pepper to taste. Mix well. Put through fine grinder twice. Put in large bowl and add eggs, parsley, matzo meal. Mix well. Add cream slowly until well absorbed. Mold fish paste into oblong fat pieces at least six inches long. Arrange in buttered saucepan. Add sliced carrots. Put 1 slice peeled lemon on each piece of fish. Cover with fish stock. Simmer slowly 25 minutes. Remove from heat. Cool. Refrigerate until jellied. Serve with horseradish sauce, made by mixing horseradish with finely chopped beets.

FISH STOCK — 1 QUART

Fish heads, bones and skin
3 cups water
1 cup white wine
½ cup white vinegar
1 bay leaf
1 onion, sliced

2 sprigs parsley
1 small carrot, sliced
1 tablespoon salt
¼ teaspoon thyme
12 black peppercorns

Boil all ingredients sharply for 20 minutes.

CHOPPED LIVER

8 medium onions, sliced
1¼ pounds calves' liver
1 pound chicken livers

2 hard-boiled eggs
Salt and pepper
3 tablespoons chicken fat

Sauté onions with 1 tablespoon chicken fat. Cover. Broil liver and chicken livers under grill. Put onions, liver and hard-boiled eggs through meat grinder. Add salt and pepper and 2 tablespoons chicken fat. Chop thoroughly until desired texture.

STUFFED CABBAGE

12 large cabbage leaves
¾ pound chopped beef
3 teaspoons bacon drippings
2½ cups cooked rice
1¼ teaspoons salt

½ teaspoon pepper
¼ cup green pepper, chopped
1½ tablespoons onion, minced
½ cup grated processed cheese
Tomato sauce

Scald cabbage leaves in boiling water. Drain. Brown chopped beef in bacon drippings in a skillet. Drain on absorbent paper. Combine rice, beef, salt, pepper, green pepper, onion and cheese. Mix well. Place about ⅛ cup of mixture on each cabbage leaf. Roll up. Place rolls side by side in shallow baking dish. Pour tomato sauce over all. Bake, basting occasionally, at 350° for about 40 minutes.

COLE SLAW

3½ pounds cabbage, grated coarsely
or chopped fine
1 green pepper, cut in small pieces
2 carrots, grated coarsely
½ tablespoon salt

½ cup vinegar diluted with about
¼ cup water
3 tablespoons mayonnaise
2 tablespoons sugar

Mix all together and refrigerate.

POTATO LATKES

12 large potatoes, peeled and grated
3 egg yolks, beaten
1½ tablespoons flour
1 large onion, grated
Salt

Pepper
3 egg whites, stiffly beaten
5 tablespoons butter or shortening
Applesauce or sour cream

Mix grated, well-drained potatoes with beaten egg yolks, flour, onion, salt and pepper to taste. Fold in stiffly beaten egg whites. Heat butter or shortening in frying pan until sizzling. Drop in potato mixture from spoon. Drain on absorbent paper. Serve hot with either applesauce or sour cream, sugared or not as preferred.

CHEESE BLINTZES

2 egg yolks, beaten
½ teaspoon salt
½ teaspoon sugar
1 teaspoon melted butter
2¼ cups milk
1½ cups flour
2 egg whites, stiffly beaten

FILLING
3 cups pot cheese or farmer cheese
2 tablespoons butter
2 eggs, beaten
1½ tablespoons sugar
¼ teaspoon cinnamon
Salt

Beat egg yolks with salt, sugar, butter and milk. Add flour. Stir briskly until batter is smooth. Fold in egg whites. Butter 6-inch skillet very lightly. Pour in a very thin layer of batter — just enough to cover bottom of pan, about 2 tablespoons. Cook on one side only until golden brown. Turn onto waxed paper or tablecloth. Repeat until batter is used up.

Prepare filling: Mix cheese, butter, egg, sugar, cinnamon and salt. Spoon a heaping tablespoon of filling onto cooked side of each blintz. Fold two sides into filling, then one end over other. Fry in butter until brown. Serve with thick sour cream.

LAUREL AND HARDY

OUR BETTERS

Our Better Baked Bean Dinner

Boston Baked Beans and Frankfurters

Sour Cream Cole Slaw

Potato Salad

Sour Pickles, Radishes

Peanut Brittle Ice Cream

Coffee

BOSTON BAKED BEANS AND FRANKFURTERS

2 cups navy or pea beans	½ teaspoon dry mustard
4 cups cold water	¼ teaspoon paprika
¼ pound piece fat bacon	1 scant teaspoon onion, grated
½ pound salt pork, scored	8 frankfurters, sliced
½ cup molasses	

Pick over beans and put in pot with cold water to soak overnight. Keep in cool place. In the morning, if any water remains, drain off and reserve. Add fresh cold water to cover. Cook beans over gentle heat in tightly covered pot. Simmer 1 hour. Drain. Reserve the water.

Put bacon in bottom of earthenware bean pot and pour in beans. Bury salt pork in center. Mix molasses with equal quantity of the bean water, mustard, paprika and grated onion. Pour over the beans. Lift them carefully with spoon so that seasoning will mix through pot.

Cover and bake in slow (300°) oven 6 hours. Once each hour add a little of the bean water, gently stirring so that water will go to bottom of pot. Surface of water in pot should always be even with beans. If there is too much water, drain and set aside. If there is too little, add more bean water.

During last hour of cooking, remove lid of bean pot so that pork on surface may become crisp and brown. Add frankfurters for the last half hour.

SOUR CREAM COLE SLAW

1 head cabbage, shredded
Thin tomato slices, peeled
1½ cups mayonnaise
1 tablespoon celery, finely chopped
1 tablespoon pimiento, finely chopped
1 tablespoon green onion, finely chopped
1 tablespoon green chervil, finely chopped
2 scant teaspoons chili powder
½ cup sour cream

Add celery, pimiento, green onion and chervil to mayonnaise. Stir in chili powder and sour cream. Pour over cabbage. Toss well. Arrange on platter. Cover with tomato slices. Top with more dressing. Chill thoroughly.

POTATO SALAD

8 boiled potatoes, peeled	3 tablespoons onion, chopped
½ cup mayonnaise	1 tablespoon onion, grated
6 tablespoons salad oil	1½ teaspoons salt
3 tablespoons tarragon vinegar	2 tablespoons parsley, chopped
3 tablespoons lemon juice	½ teaspoon pepper, freshly ground

Mix sliced potatoes with mayonnaise in a casserole. Season with oil, vinegar, lemon juice, onions and salt. Sprinkle with parsley and pepper. Mix carefully. Serve well chilled.

PEANUT BRITTLE ICE CREAM

½ teaspoon gelatin
2 tablespoons cold water
1 cup evaporated milk, undiluted
1 cup peanut brittle
1½ teaspoons vanilla

Soften gelatin in cold water. Scald milk in top of double boiler. Add softened gelatin. Stir until dissolved. Chill until very cold. Grind peanut brittle, using finest blade of food grinder. Whip chilled milk until stiff. Fold in peanut brittle and vanilla. Freeze, without stirring, in freezer tray at coldest setting.

GRETA GARBO AND JOHN GILBERT

QUEEN CHRISTINA

Swedish Smörgåsbord

Jellied Salmon

Herring Salad

Salt Herring with New Potatoes

Pickled Cucumbers

Boiled Lamb with Dill Sauce

Meatballs

Anchovies and Potatoes

Radishes, tomatoes, olives and onions

Two or three different kinds of bread

Boiled Sliced Ham

Fruit Compote

JELLIED SALMON

4 cups celery stalks and tops, coarsely chopped
1½ teaspoons dried dill
1 onion, peeled
4-pound piece of salmon
2 quarts water
1 bay leaf
½ teaspoon whole allspice
1 teaspoon white pepper
4 teaspoons salt
3 envelopes (3 tablespoons) unflavored gelatin
Watercress
Lemon wedges

Make a Court Bouillon: Place celery with dill, onion and fish in large kettle. Add water. Add bay leaf, allspice, pepper and salt. Bring to boil. Simmer until fish is tender. Cool. Remove skin and bones. Strain court bouillon. Taste. Add salt if needed.

Soften gelatin in ¾ cup cool court bouillon. Heat ¾ cup of the remaining bouillon. Stir in softened gelatin. Line large fish-shaped mold with larger pieces of fish, and fill in the center with flaked pieces. Pour in bouillon and chill. Unmold on large plate and garnish with sprigs of watercress and lemon wedges, arranged spoke fashion.

You may mold this jellied salmon in a fish mold and decorate it with olive rings and strips of pimiento.

HERRING SALAD

1 fillet of salt herring, soaked overnight in cold water
1½ cups boiled potatoes
1½ cups pickled beets
½ cup apples
¼ cup onion
⅓ cup pickled gherkins
4 tablespoons vinegar
2 tablespoons water
2 tablespoons sugar
White pepper to taste
½ cup whipped cream
1 or 2 hard-boiled eggs
Parsley
1 cup sour cream
3 teaspoons beet juice (optional)

Dice fillet, potatoes, beets, apples, onion and gherkins. Mix thoroughly. Blend vinegar, water, sugar and pepper. Add ½ cup whipped cream. Pour on fillet-potato mixture. Chill in refrigerator. Serve garnished with hard-boiled eggs and parsley. Serve with sour cream colored, if desired, with beet juice.

SALT HERRING WITH NEW POTATOES

1 large jar marinated herring
1 tablespoon chives, chopped
1 small onion, sliced paper-thin
1 cup sour cream

Sprinkle herring with chopped chives and onion. Mix with chilled sour cream. Serve garnished with chopped chives.

PICKLED CUCUMBERS

2 small cucumbers
½ cup vinegar
2 tablespoons water
2 tablespoons sugar

¼ teaspoon salt
Dash white pepper
1 tablespoon parsley, chopped

Slice unpeeled cucumber. Discard ends. Mix vinegar, water, sugar, salt and white pepper thoroughly. Pour over cucumber. Sprinkle with parsley. Allow to stand 2 to 3 hours in refrigerator before serving.

BOILED LAMB WITH DILL SAUCE

2 to 2½ pounds breast or shoulder
    of lamb
3 or 4 white peppercorns

1 bay leaf
1 tablespoon dill sprigs, chopped, or
    ½ teaspoon dill seeds

Rinse meat quickly with hot water. Place in kettle. Cover with boiling salted water. Bring to boil. Skim. Add bay leaf, dill, salt and pepper. Cover. Simmer 1½ hours until tender. Cut in pieces. Garnish with fresh dill. Serve with dill sauce and boiled potatoes.

DILL SAUCE

2 tablespoons butter
2 tablespoons flour
2 cups stock
2 tablespoons fresh dill, chopped, or
    1 teaspoon dill seeds

1½ tablespoons vinegar
½ to 1 tablespoon sugar
Salt
1 egg yolk

Melt butter, add flour. Stir until well blended. Add stock gradually. Stir constantly. Cook slowly 10 minutes. Stir occasionally. Add dill, vinegar and sugar. Season to taste. Remove from heat. Cool slightly. Stir in beaten egg yolk.

MEATBALLS

½ pound beef, ground	1 egg
¼ pound veal, ground	1½ teaspoons salt
¼ pound pork, ground	¼ teaspoon white pepper
3 tablespoons onion, chopped	1 tablespoon flour
6 tablespoons butter	¾ to 1 cup cream or milk
½ cup bread crumbs	Salt
1½ cups milk	White pepper

Sauté onion in 1 tablespoon melted butter until golden brown. Soak bread crumbs in milk. Add meat, egg, onion, salt and pepper. Mix thoroughly until smooth. Shape into walnut-size balls, using 2 tablespoons dipped in cold water. Fry in butter until evenly brown. Shake continuously to keep balls round. Remove each batch to saucepan and keep warm. Clear skillet with a little water before adding next batch. Reserve pan juice each time. Then: Mix flour, cream and pan juices. Stir constantly. Simmer 10 minutes. Add more milk or cream if too thick. Season. Place meatballs in serving dish with gravy.

ANCHOVIES AND POTATOES

20 Swedish anchovy fillets	4 or 5 medium-size raw potatoes,
2 onions, sliced	peeled and cut in strings
3 tablespoons butter	1½ cups cream

Sauté sliced onions in 1 tablespoon butter. Place potatoes, onions and anchovy fillets in alternate layers in buttered baking dish, finishing with layer of potatoes. Add a little juice from anchovy can. Dot with remaining butter. Bake in moderately hot (400°) oven. Add ¾ cup cream after 10 minutes, and remainder after another 10 minutes. Then reduce heat to 300°. Bake another 20 minutes, until potatoes are soft.

FRUIT COMPOTE

2 cups water
¾ cup sugar
6 small peaches
6 apricots
6 greengage plums
½ cup orange sections, free of pith
    and membranes

¼ cup seedless grapes
¼ cup sliced bananas
¼ cup melon balls
Orange rind, shredded and blanched

Bring water and sugar to boil. Skim carefully. Plunge peaches and apricots into boiling water for a second or two, and then into cold water. Slip off skins. Wash plums. Add peaches, apricots and plums to the syrup. Cover. Simmer very slowly 10 minutes until fruit is tender. Cool. Chill fruit in syrup. Combine orange sections, grapes, bananas and melon balls. Add to the chilled fruit. Serve garnished with shredded orange rind. Serve very cold.

BORIS KARLOFF

THE BRIDE OF FRANKENSTEIN

Monster American Breakfast

Half and Half
(ORANGE AND GRAPEFRUIT JUICE)

*Eggs Benedict with Broiled Ham Slices
on English Muffin*

Daisy Chain (see page 119) and Buckwheat Cakes

Home Fried Potatoes

Strawberries and Cream

EGGS BENEDICT

12 eggs
12 thin slices cooked ham
12 buttered, toasted English muffins, cut in half
1 cup Hollandaise Sauce

Poach eggs in an egg poacher or large skillet. While eggs are poaching, make Hollandaise Sauce (see page 29). When eggs have finished cooking, place piece of ham on each buttered muffin round. Top each with a poached egg. Top with Hollandaise Sauce.

HOME FRIED POTATOES

3 cups boiled potatoes, diced
3 tablespoons butter
3 small onions, diced

Sauté potatoes in butter over medium heat until golden brown. Remove and set aside. Add onions to the pan. Cook until transparent. Add more butter if necessary. Return potatoes to pan and mix with onions. Cook all together, pressing down on the mixture with a spatula. Cook until crisp brown on both sides.

LUISE RAINER AND PAUL MUNI

THE GOOD EARTH

Good Earth Food

Peking Doilies

Chicken and Pineapple

Steamed Roast Pork Buns

Steamed Cantonese Fish

Boiled Rice

Iced Kumquats, Pineapple and Shredded Coconut

PEKING DOILIES

5 cups flour
1 tablespoon salt

2 cups boiling water
¼ cup peanut oil

Mix salt in flour. Place in deep bowl. Pour in boiling water. Stir quickly until all flour is dampened. Place dough on pastry board and knead until smooth. Add more hot water or flour if necessary to make a stiff dough. Roll out 1 inch thick. Cut into 2-inch strips. Cut strips into squares. Flatten each square slightly on floured board. Smear on a little oil. Place 2 pieces together and roll out very thin, keeping the shape round. Place 1 round at a time on a hot slightly greased frying pan. Cook 1 minute. Turn and cook until both sides are done.

FILLING

1 cup each: roast pork, finely sliced
　　　　　cooked chicken meat, finely sliced
　　　　　roast duck meat, finely sliced
　　　　　cooked ham, finely sliced
　　　　　bean sprouts, warmed in 2 tablespoons peanut oil
　　　　　cabbage, peeled and finely sliced
1 egg, beaten, fried like a thin pancake and then shredded
1 cucumber, peeled and finely sliced
1 stalk spring onion, parboiled and sliced

Arrange sliced meat in separate portions on large plate. Place in middle of table. Put prepared vegetables and sauce (small plate of soy sauce mixed with tomato catsup, spiked with Tabasco) in individual plates around meat.

Each person serves himself: Place some sauce on doily, add a tablespoonful of meat and vegetable in center. Fold ends together to make a roll. Season with soy sauce to taste.

CHICKEN AND PINEAPPLE

2 chickens, each about 2 pounds,
　　cut up
½ cup flour
½ teaspoon pepper, freshly ground
9 tablespoons salad oil

½ cup soy sauce
5 green peppers, cut into strips
5 medium onions, chopped
¾ cup crushed pineapple

Dredge chicken in flour mixed with pepper. Brown on both sides in 3 tablespoons of oil. Add soy sauce. Cover. Cook 10 minutes. Remove chicken.

Heat remaining oil. Add green peppers and onions. Cook until pepper is softened. Return chicken to pan. Add pineapple. Cover. Cook until chicken is tender.

STEAMED ROAST PORK BUNS

1 pound roast pork, cut into cubes and seasoned with oyster sauce	4 teaspoons baking powder
5 cups self-rising flour	2 tablespoons white vinegar
1 cup fine sugar	⅜ cup lard
	1⅓ cup cold water

Mix flour, sugar, baking powder, vinegar, lard and water to form soft dough. Knead 10 minutes. Cut into strips. Roll like sausages 1½ inches wide in diameter. Break off small pieces of dough the size of a walnut. Flatten each piece. Fill with seasoned meat. Form into dumplings. Place each on a small square of waxed paper. Put 1 inch apart in steamer. Steam over rapidly boiling water 20 minutes. Serve hot.

STEAMED CANTONESE FISH

3-pound whole, very fresh sea bass. (The fish must be fresh.)	3 very thin slices green ginger root or 2 teaspoons powdered ginger
1½ teaspoons salt	½ teaspoon powdered cinnamon
3 tablespoons soy sauce	4 slender scallions, cut in long pieces and split
½ lemon peel, shredded thin as hair or grated	¾ cup cooking oil

Pour boiling water into preheated oval pan about same size as fish. Lower fish into water. There must be enough water to cover fish. Let it stand covered 25 minutes. When fish eyes pop up, half out, fish is cooked. Remove gently from water onto a warm oval platter. Sprinkle with salt. Sprinkle remaining ingredients over it. Heat oil. Pour over fish and serve immediately.

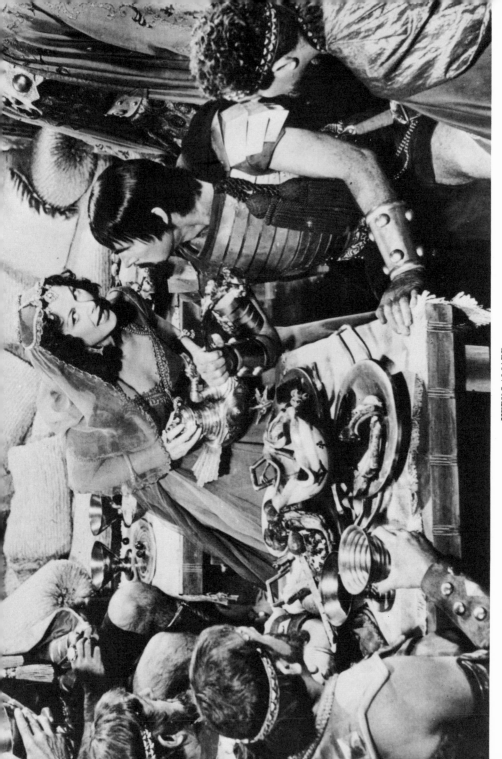

HEDY LAMARR

SAMSON AND DELILAH

Middle East Dinner

Yogurt Soup

Stuffed Grape Leaves with Avgolemono Sauce

Shish Kebab

Samson's Temptation
(ARABIC RICE)

Hearts of Palm Salad

Sesame Seeds and Honey

Halvah

Delilah's Delight
(TURKISH FRUIT SALAD)

YOGURT SOUP

½ cup pearl barley
4 cups broth or 2 cans bouillon and
   1 can water
1 teaspoon salt
½ teaspoon pepper

2 cups yogurt
1 cup sour cream
1 egg, well beaten
4 tablespoons butter, melted
2 tablespoons parsley, chopped

Soak barley overnight in water to cover. Drain well. Combine with broth, salt and pepper. Cook in a saucepan over low heat for 2 hours or until barley is soft. Beat yogurt, sour cream and egg in a bowl. Gradually add 1 cup of the soup, beating constantly to prevent curdling. Add remaining soup, beating constantly. Add butter and parsley. Mix well. Correct seasoning. Reheat but do not allow to boil.

STUFFED GRAPE LEAVES WITH AVGOLEMONO SAUCE

1½ pounds meat, chopped
8 large onions, finely chopped
1 cup raw rice
Salt and pepper to taste
½ teaspoon dried mint leaves

1 cup water
1-pound jar grape leaves
2 to 3 cups bouillon
1 tablespoon water

Combine meat, onions, rice, salt, pepper and mint. Add water. Mix well. Drain jar of grape leaves. Remove leaves. Wash well to remove all traces of brine. Put heaping tablespoons of meat mixture in center of each leaf. Roll leaf tightly. Fold edges over (rolling toward point of leaf). Place torn leaves on bottom of buttered casserole. Arrange stuffed leaves in layers. Add enough bouillon to cover. Dot with butter. Cover with a heavy plate to keep rolls from opening as rice cooks. Cover casserole. Put a weight on top. Steam over low heat for 1 hour. If there is no liquid when cooked, add bouillon and simmer for a few minutes longer.

SAUCE

3 eggs, well beaten
Juice of 1 lemon
Hot gravy, about 4 tablespoons

Beat lemon juice into eggs. Beat again. Add some of hot gravy from grape leaves casserole. Pour egg mixture over stuffed leaves. Serve at once. If necessary to reheat, warm very slowly, uncovered, in order not to curdle egg sauce.

SHISH KEBAB

2 pounds tender lamb, cut in 1½-inch squares
Juice of 2 large lemons
4 tablespoons olive oil
2 tablespoons onion, grated
2 tablespoons chili peppers, ground
1 teaspoon coriander
1 teaspoon powdered ginger

1 clove garlic, mashed to a pulp
2 teaspoons turmeric
2 teaspoons curry powder
3 teaspoons salt
Slices of tomato, onion, green pepper and mushroom caps cut approximately the same size
Melted butter

Marinate lamb about 2 hours in a mixture of lemon juice, olive oil, onion, chili peppers, coriander, ginger, garlic, turmeric, curry powder and salt.

Thread meat on skewers, alternating with tomato, onion, green pepper and mushroom caps. Broil *kebabs* under hot broiler. Turn and brown all sides. Baste often with melted butter. Serve with wild rice.

SAMSON'S TEMPTATION
(Arabic Rice)

5 tablespoons butter
1 cup pine nuts
2 cups broken extra-fine vermicelli
 — if possible, *capellini d'angelo*

2 cups rice
4 cups seasoned bouillon, heated
2 cups raisins, plumped

In a saucepan, sauté pine nuts in 3 tablespoons butter until just brown. Remove and set aside. Add 1 tablespoon butter to pan and sauté *capellini d'angelo* pieces until brown. Set aside. Add 1 tablespoon butter to pan and stir in rice until it takes on color. Pour in hot bouillon. Cover tightly. Cook until tender — about 12 to 15 minutes. Mix in pine nuts, plumped raisins and *capellini d'angelo* and serve.

HEARTS OF PALM SALAD

Arrange slices of hearts of palm lengthwise on a large serving plate. Serve with French dressing mixed with a little chopped watercress.

DELILAH'S DELIGHT

(Turkish Fruit Salad)

- 2 teaspoons powdered ginger
- ½ cup brandy
- 2 oranges, peeled and thinly sliced
- 1 peach, peeled and sliced
- 1 cup fresh or canned pineapple, cubed
- 1 cup strawberries, hulled and halved

Dissolve ginger in brandy. Combine oranges, peach, pineapple and strawberries. Pour brandy over the fruit. Mix well. Cover. Chill for about 3 hours. Arrange on lettuce leaves to serve.

HOLD THAT BLONDE

Magnolia Dinner

Hush Puppy Stew
(LAMB WITH CARROTS, POTATOES, CELERY AND PEAS)

Hush Puppies

Onion and Tomato Salad Savannah

Maple Mousse and Pralines

EDDIE BRACKEN AND VERONICA LAKE

HUSH PUPPY STEW
(Lamb Stew)

2 pounds lamb (shoulder, breast or
  flank)
3 tablespoons flour
2 tablespoons fat
1 small onion, sliced
¼ cup diced celery
2 tablespoons parsley, chopped
3 cups boiling broth or water
½ teaspoon Worcestershire

1 bay leaf
1 teaspoon salt
¼ teaspoon pepper
2 tablespoons prepared mustard
4 carrots, diced
6 tiny whole potatoes, peeled
1 cup sliced celery
1 cup fresh peas

Cut lamb into 2-inch pieces. Flour well and brown in fat. Add onion, diced celery, parsley, water and seasoning. Cover and simmer for 1½ hours. Skim off any excess fat. Add carrots, potatoes, sliced celery and peas. Simmer 30 minutes.

HUSH PUPPIES

¾ cup white corn meal
¼ cup flour
1 tablespoon baking powder
¼ teaspoon salt
1 teaspoon sugar

1 egg
6 tablespoons milk
2 tablespoons onion, chopped
Shortening

Sift corn meal, flour, baking powder, salt and sugar. Beat egg into milk and onion. Stir into the corn meal mixture all at once. Drop by spoonfuls into deep hot shortening. Fry until golden brown. Drain on absorbent paper. Serve hot. Makes 12 hush puppies.

ONION AND TOMATO SALAD SAVANNAH

1 large Spanish onion, thinly sliced
6 large tomatoes, peeled and thickly sliced
2 tablespoons chives, chopped
2 tablespoons basil, chopped
2 tablespoons dill, chopped
1 teaspoon poppy seeds
½ teaspoon sugar
¾ teaspoon salt
Dash freshly ground pepper

Arrange onion rings on the bottom of a large bowl. Cover with tomato slices. Sprinkle with chives, basil, dill, poppy seeds, sugar, salt and pepper. Chill thoroughly.

MAPLE MOUSSE

1⅓ cups maple syrup
4 eggs, separated
Pinch salt
1 cup heavy cream, whipped
1 teaspoon lemon juice

Bring syrup to a boil. Skim. Beat egg yolks until thick. Stir syrup very slowly into the eggs. Cook in double boiler until thickened. Stir constantly. Remove from heat. Beat egg whites with salt. Fold in whipped cream. Add lemon juice. Pour into freezer trays or shallow serving bowl. Freeze until mushy. Stir once. Refreeze until firm.

PRALINES

2 cups sugar
1 cup cream
1 cup pecans

Mix sugar with cream. Cook on very low heat until a drop will become a soft ball in a cup of cool water. Remove from heat. Add pecans. Beat well. Spoon onto aluminum foil. Cool.

MEET ME IN ST. LOUIS

Thanksgiving Dinner

Cream of Watercress Soup

Roast Turkey Missouri Style

Chestnut and Oyster Stuffing

Creamed Pumpkin Amandine

Artichokes with Peas

Tomatoes Grégoire

Orange and Olive Salad

Strawberries with Chocolate and Rum

Mincemeat Pie

JUDY GARLAND

CREAM OF WATERCRESS SOUP

¼ cup butter
1 leek, chopped
½ cup onion, chopped
1 quart potatoes, thinly sliced
1 tablespoon salt
¼ teaspoon black pepper, freshly ground

1 cup water
1 bunch watercress
2 cups milk
1 cup water
2 egg yolks
½ cup heavy cream

Sauté leek and onion in butter until tender. Add potatoes, salt, pepper and water. Cover. Bring to a boil. Reduce heat. Simmer until potatoes are almost tender.

Mince watercress stems. Chop leaves coarsely. (Set some aside for garnishing.) Add watercress to potato mixture. Stir in milk and 1 cup water. Cook 15 minutes.

Purée the soup in an electric blender with egg yolks, then add cream. Reheat. Do not boil. Serve garnished with chopped watercress leaves.

ROAST TURKEY MISSOURI STYLE

1 turkey
Salt
Water
Softened butter
Stuffing

Rub turkey inside and out with salt. Fill neck and body with stuffing. Fasten cavities with poultry pins and lace with cord. Fasten legs to sides of bird. Wrap in a tight covering of aluminum foil. Put breast side down in roasting pan for first hour of roasting. Turn it breast side up for the rest of the time. Have a small quantity of water in the bottom of roasting pan at all times. Allow 22 minutes a pound in a moderate (350°) oven. Test by inserting a skewer into the fleshy part of thigh. If skewer goes in easily and juice that flows out is clear and not pink, the bird is cooked. Remove foil about ½ hour before finish and brush well with softened butter. Brown in hot (400°) oven. Brush several times with butter. The skin will be crisp and golden brown. Make gravy from the pan drippings.

CHESTNUT AND OYSTER STUFFING

You may make stuffing the day before and refrigerate, BUT — *do not* stuff bird until time to roast.

6 cups bread cubes, lightly toasted
1 small onion, finely chopped
1½ cups celery, finely chopped
2 cups cooked dried chestnuts, coarsely chopped
10 medium-sized oysters, coarsely chopped
1 Shredded Wheat biscuit, crushed

1½ teaspoons Worcestershire
1 clove garlic, crushed
1 teaspoon salt
½ teaspoon poultry seasoning
¼ teaspoon each rosemary, thyme and marjoram
⅛ teaspoon pepper
½ cup butter, melted

Soak chestnuts overnight in warm water. Drain. Cover with water. Boil 1 hour until tender. Mix bread cubes with onion and celery. Add chestnuts, oysters, Shredded Wheat and remaining seasonings. Mix in melted butter. This stuffing is enough for a 10 to 14 pound turkey.

CREAMED PUMPKIN AMANDINE

4 cups cooked pumpkin, cut in small cubes
2½ or more cups cream sauce, well-seasoned
3 tablespoons melted butter
¾ cup almonds, blanched and shredded

Combine pumpkin with cream sauce. Taste for seasoning. Pour into baking dish. Brush top with melted butter. Sprinkle with almonds. Brown quickly under broiler until almonds are golden. Serve immediately.

ARTICHOKES WITH PEAS

3 medium-sized artichokes
Boiling salted water
Juice of 1 lemon
1 box frozen peas
1 canned pimiento, sliced

Cut tips off artichokes. Cut in half lengthwise. Scoop out choke. Cook in boiling salted water with lemon juice until tender — about 45 minutes. Heat peas. Drain. Fill cavities of artichokes with peas. Garnish with pimiento strips.

TOMATOES GRÉGOIRE

18 to 20 small fresh-peeled Italian tomatoes
4 tablespoons sugar

Place tomatoes in small, very well buttered baking dish. Sprinkle with sugar. Bake in hot (425°) oven 30 minutes.

ORANGE AND OLIVE SALAD

2 large oranges, skin and pith removed, cut in paper-thin quarters
Romaine lettuce

6 thin slices red onion, separated into rings
12 black olives, pitted and sliced
French dressing

Toss oranges in salad bowl with torn lettuce leaves. Add onion and olives. Toss again with French dressing.

STRAWBERRIES WITH CHOCOLATE AND RUM

1 quart whole strawberries, hulled
½ cup granulated sugar
1 cup heavy cream, whipped
½ cup sweet chocolate, grated

1 tablespoon confectioners' sugar
1½ tablespoons light rum
2 tablespoons grated orange rind

Sprinkle strawberries with granulated sugar. Chill in refrigerator until ready to serve.

Fold chocolate and confectioners' sugar into whipped cream. Stir in rum. Pour over chilled strawberries. Top with orange rind.

MINCEMEAT PIE

1 box pie crust mix
1 quart prepared mincemeat, mixed with 1 jigger brandy

Prepare 2 pie crusts as directed on package. Place 1 in 9-inch pie plate. Fill with heated mincemeat and brandy. Cover with other half of pastry. Crimp edges together. Bake according to package directions and until crust is lightly browned.

CLAUDETTE COLBERT

CLEOPATRA

Cleopatra Dinner

Lemon Soup

Eggplant Caviar

Moussaka à la Turque

Aswan Salad
(MIXED TOMATO, CUCUMBER AND SWEET PEPPER SALAD)

Cherries Jubilee

Turkish Coffee

LEMON SOUP

4 cans chicken broth plus water to make six cups broth
3 tablespoons uncooked rice
3 eggs, beaten
3 tablespoons lemon juice

Cook rice in simmering broth until tender, about 20 minutes. Beat eggs until light, and gradually add lemon juice, beating until blended. Mix half of the hot soup slowly into the egg mixture, stirring constantly. Add remaining soup. Do not heat again. If it should curdle, add one egg yolk and beat with rotary beater. Serve at once.

EGGPLANT CAVIAR

1 large eggplant
4 tomatoes, skinned and finely chopped
1 onion, grated

1 onion, finely chopped
6 cloves garlic, crushed
¾ cup olive oil
Salt and black pepper

Brush a piece of aluminum foil well with oil. Wrap around eggplant and bake until soft in a 350° oven about 30 minutes. Meanwhile, mix tomatoes, onions, garlic and salt. Unwrap the eggplant. Carefully remove skin and mash meat very fine. Add tomato mixture. Continue mashing, slowly adding olive oil, salt and pepper. When very fine and well mixed, set in refrigerator until very cold. Serve surrounded by crushed ice with fingers of hot buttered toast.

MOUSSAKA À LA TURQUE

3½ cups shoulder of lamb, ground left-over or freshly cooked
3 medium-size eggplants
4 tablespoons olive oil
4 tablespoons butter
2 onions, finely chopped
1 clove garlic, chopped

2 medium-sized tomatoes, peeled and chopped
¼ teaspoon basil
2 tablespoons parsley, chopped
Salt and pepper
2 eggs, beaten
Tomato sauce

Put lamb through meat grinder to make 3½ cups. Cut eggplants in two lengthwise. Sauté meat side down in olive oil over moderate heat for 5 minutes. Add more olive oil if necessary. Scoop out eggplant meat, leaving skins intact. Chop eggplant meat fine and blend with ground lamb.

Heat butter in a large skillet. Add onions and garlic. Sauté mixture until transparent and lightly colored. Add lamb-eggplant mixture and continue to cook until eggplant is soft. Stir frequently. Add tomatoes, basil, parsley, salt and pepper to taste. Cook over moderate heat about 5 minutes. Mix well. Add eggs. Mix again.

Oil sides and bottom of timbale mold. Line it with eggplant skins overlapping, purple sides down and with half the skins hanging out of the mold so that they may be folded over the filling later. Fill with meat-vegetable mixture and fold the skins up and around so they will meet in the center over the top. Place mold in a larger pan of hot water and bake in moderate (375°) oven for 45 minutes, or until firm. Remove from oven, allow to set for a few minutes. Unmold onto a heated platter. Surround the *moussaka* with tomato sauce.

ASWAN SALAD

3 tomatoes, cubed
2 cucumbers, peeled and diced
1 green pepper, chopped
8 scallions, sliced thin
4 tablespoons parsley, chopped
4 sprigs fresh mint, chopped, or
   1 tablespoon dried mint

½ cup olive oil
¼ cup lemon juice
1 teaspoon onion, grated
1 teaspoon salt
2 cups bread cubes, as small as
   possible

Combine tomatoes, cucumbers, green pepper, scallions, parsley and mint in a bowl. Mix olive oil, lemon juice, onion and salt together. Pour over vegetables. Add bread cubes. Toss lightly. Chill for 1 hour before serving.

CHERRIES JUBILEE

1 tablespoon cornstarch
1 tablespoon sugar
1 cup juice from canned
   Bing cherries

1 tablespoon lemon juice
2 cups canned Bing cherries, pitted
½ cup brandy or Kirsch
Vanilla ice cream

Mix cornstarch, sugar and cherry juice slowly, stirring until smooth. Cook in a chafing dish over low heat, stirring constantly, until the sauce reaches boiling point and is slightly thickened. Stir in lemon juice. Add cherries and remove from heat. Pour warmed brandy or Kirsch over sauce and cherries. Light with match and carry to the table flaming. Serve at once over ice cream.

TURKISH COFFEE

2 cups water
6 sugar lumps
6 or 7 teaspoons extra fine ground Italian coffee

Boil water, sugar and coffee in saucepan 10 seconds. Remove from heat. Cool slightly. Repeat twice. Pour into warm demitasse cups. Allow grounds to settle before serving.

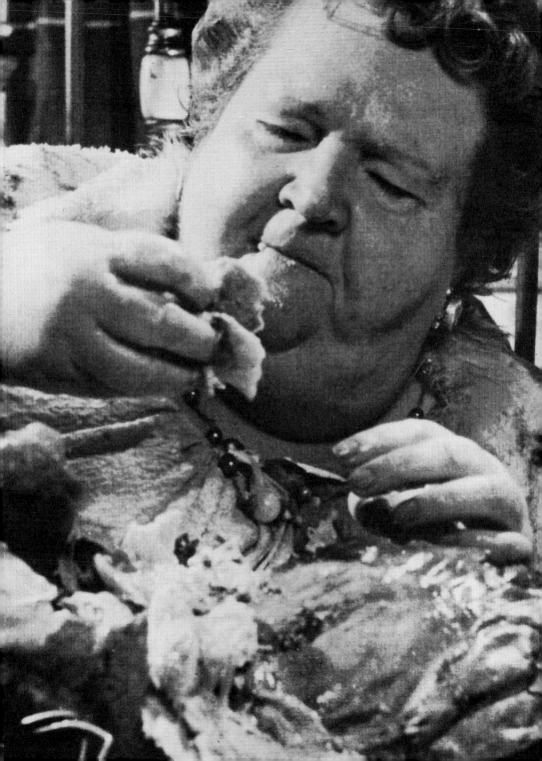

BORIS KARLOFF

FU MANCHU

Chinese Dinner Fu Manchu

Lobster Cantonese

Chicken Chow Mein

Pineapple Duck

Chinese Beef and Tomatoes

Boiled Rice

Crab Meat and Melon Soup

LOBSTER CANTONESE

3 stalks celery, finely diced
1 clove garlic, minced
1 onion, chopped
1 large carrot, finely diced
3 tablespoons oil
6 strips bacon
3 cups chicken broth

½ cup water
3 tablespoons soy sauce
2 tablespoons cornstarch
4 cups cooked lobster meat, coarsely
    chopped
2 eggs, lightly beaten
½ teaspoon pepper

Cook celery, garlic, carrot and onion slowly in very hot oil for 10 minutes in a large skillet. Then fry bacon until crisp. Drain and crumble it. Heat chicken broth. Mix water, soy sauce and cornstarch until smooth. Place lobster in skillet with celery mixture. Add bacon. Pour in chicken broth. Pour in beaten eggs. Stir constantly over low heat for 5 minutes. Gradually add cornstarch mixture. Season with black pepper. Cook another 5 minutes.

CHICKEN CHOW MEIN

4-pound chicken, disjointed
Bouquet garni: 1 bay leaf, 3 sprigs parsley,
    ½ celery stalk
2 generous tablespoons lard or cooking oil
1 large onion, thinly sliced
2 cups celery, cut into thin strips
¾ pound fresh mushrooms, peeled and sliced
1 cup fresh water chestnuts
1 cup fresh bean sprouts
¾ cup bamboo shoots
1 generous tablespoon cornstarch
3 tablespoons soy sauce
Salt and pepper
Egg noodles fried in deep fat

Cook chicken until tender in salted water with *bouquet garni*. Drain. Reserve broth. Discard *bouquet garni*. Bone chicken pieces. Return bones to broth. Simmer, covered, gently 1 hour. Cut meat into thin strips, reserving white meat for garnishing.

Brown onion in cooking oil in a large skillet over low heat. Stir in celery and mushrooms. Add 1 cup strained chicken broth. Simmer gently 10 minutes. Stir occasionally. Stir in water chestnuts, bean sprouts and bamboo shoots.

Mix cornstarch with ½ cup strained chicken broth and soy sauce. Stir into frying pan until well mixed. Add chicken meat. Simmer 10 minutes. Season with salt, pepper and soy sauce. Serve on egg noodles. Garnish with strips of breast meat.

PINEAPPLE DUCK

Breast and thigh meat from 1 roast duck
½ fresh pineapple, peeled and cut in chunks
1 Spanish onion
1 small piece fresh ginger or 4 pieces candied ginger

¾ teaspoon salt
2 teaspoons sugar
¼ cup white vinegar
¼ cup sesame seeds
1 tablespoon English mustard
1 tablespoon water
1 tablespoon salad oil

Cut onion and ginger into fine shreds. Add ½ teaspoon salt. Marinate 10 minutes. Add mixture of 1½ teaspoons sugar and 3 tablespoons vinegar to marinade. Marinate another 30 minutes.

Toast sesame seeds in small frying pan over very low heat. Stir constantly. If heat becomes too great and seeds start popping, remove pan from heat for a moment. Toast seeds to light golden. Cool. Crush gently with rolling pin.

Mix English mustard, 1 tablespoon vinegar and ½ teaspoon sugar with 1 tablespoon water. Stir constantly until mustard actually begins to smell hot. Cover. Set aside.

Cut duck into ⅛-inch-thick slices. Add ¼ teaspoon salt, mustard mixture and crushed sesame seeds. Drain ginger and onions. Add to duck mixture. Sprinkle with 1 tablespoon salad oil. Add pineapple chunks, mix together thoroughly and serve. If candied ginger is used, add more vinegar to taste.

CHINESE BEEF AND TOMATOES

1½ pounds round steak, cut paper-thin
¼ cup plus 3 tablespoons soy sauce
1 teaspoon sugar
1 clove garlic, crushed
¾ teaspoon ginger

¼ cup salad oil
2 green peppers, seeded and cut into julienne strips
3 large tomatoes, peeled and cut into eighths
2 teaspoons cornstarch

Marinate meat in a mixture of ¼ cup soy sauce and sugar for ½ hour. Meanwhile, cook garlic and ginger in oil for a few minutes. Add green peppers. Sauté, stirring constantly, for a few minutes. Add beef and liquid. Cook another few minutes. Add tomatoes. Cover. Simmer a few minutes until tomatoes are hot. Blend cornstarch with 3 tablespoons soy sauce. Stir into mixture. Cook 1 minute more until thickened.

CRAB MEAT AND MELON SOUP

1 can crab chunks
1 honeydew melon
2 slices ham, cut in strips
Pork bones to make broth

1 tablespoon soy sauce
4 tablespoons salt
1 egg, beaten
1 teaspoon cornstarch

Make 1½ quarts broth from pork bones and ham strips. Cut melon into large pieces and boil in water to cover until soft. Remove melon from water. Scrape out pulp. Place pulp and crab meat in a saucepan. Sprinkle with salt. Add broth with ham (after removing pork bones). Bring to boiling point. Combine cornstarch with a little water and soy sauce. Stir mixture into hot broth until of desired consistency. Beat egg well and add to hot soup just before serving.

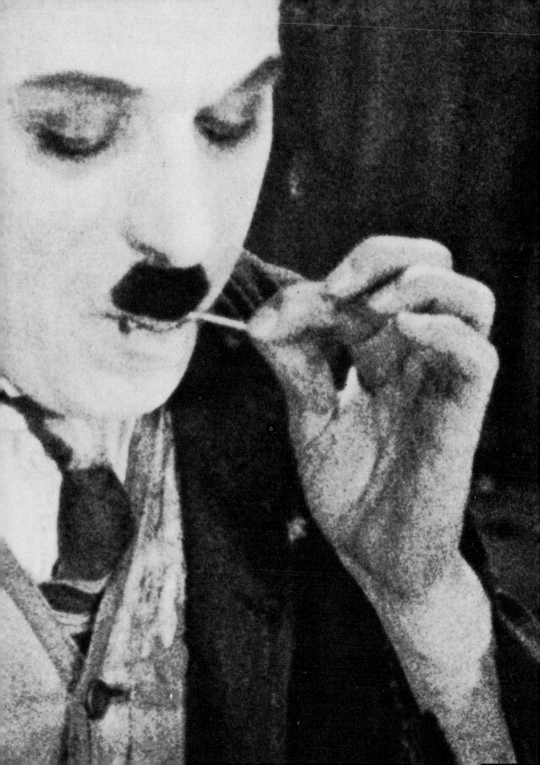

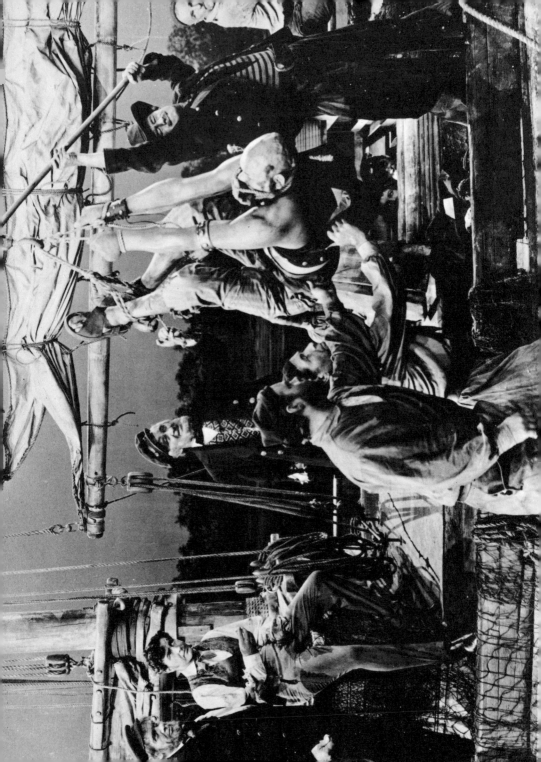

REAP THE WILD WIND

Petite Marmite Dinner

Petite Marmite
(BEEF AND VEGETABLE SOUP)

Green salad with assorted cheeses

Brandied Strawberries Alexander

PETITE MARMITE
(Beef and Vegetable Soup)

4 pounds rump of beef
1 veal knuckle
4 pounds beef bones
4½ quarts water
3 chicken bouillon cubes
Salt
4 peppercorns
1 large white turnip, diced
¼ yellow turnip, diced
3 carrots, diced

6 small leeks, sliced
2 stalks celery, diced
1 large onion stuck with 3 whole cloves
1 small head cabbage, cut in 6 wedges
½ bay leaf
½ teaspoon thyme
Thin slices dry toast
Parmesan cheese, grated

Place beef, veal knuckle and bones in large soup kettle with water, chicken bouillon cubes, salt and peppercorns. Bring water to boil. Cook gently for 2 hours. Skim surface frequently. Add turnips, carrots, leeks, celery, onion and cabbage. Add bay leaf and thyme. Cook soup for 1½ hours. Cool. Remove fat from surface. Correct seasoning. Reheat and serve.

The meat, vegetables and broth may be put all together into a soup tureen — or the soup may be served as a first course, followed by the sliced meat and vegetables. Serve with thin slices of French bread. It may also be served in small individual casseroles. Top each with a thin slice of dry toast. Sprinkle with grated Parmesan cheese. Place under broiler flame until browned.

BRANDIED STRAWBERRIES ALEXANDER

1 pint whipping cream
1 quart vanilla ice cream
2 wineglasses curaçao
3 wineglasses brandy
1 quart washed and hulled straw-
    berries, crushed
1 quart strawberries, halved

Whip cream and mix with ice cream. Add curaçao and brandy. Mix well. Blend in crushed strawberries plus half of the halved ones. Top with remaining strawberries. Work quickly to prevent mixture from becoming too mushy. If not served immediately, place in freezer until 15 minutes before serving.

RONALD COLMAN AND MARGO

LOST HORIZON

Shangri-La Dinner

Shrimp Balls in Curry Sauce

Meat Curry

Chicken Curry

Orange Rice

Rice and Shrimp

Seasoned Yogurt

Carrot Sweet Kheer

SHRIMP BALLS IN CURRY SAUCE

3 cups (3 cans, 5 ounces each) cooked, deveined shrimps
1 tablespoon minced onion
2 eggs
1 teaspoon ground coriander
½ teaspoon ground cumin seeds
½ teaspoon powdered mustard
½ teaspoon ground turmeric
1 teaspoon salt (eliminate salt if canned shrimp is used)
⅛ teaspoon garlic powder
3 tablespoons flour
⅓ cup water
Vegetable shortening
¼ cup evaporated milk or coconut milk
1 teaspoon fresh lemon juice

Put shrimp and onion through food chopper twice, using finest blade. Blend in eggs, spices and flour. Mix until almost pastelike consistency. Add water and cook 5 minutes, until mixture almost sticks to pan. Shape into balls 1½ inch in diameter. Brown in melted shortening. Drain. Add Curry Sauce. Cook gently 5 minutes. Add milk and heat 1 to 2 minutes. Do not stir, to prevent breaking shrimp balls. Add lemon juice and serve on rice.

CURRY SAUCE

⅓ cup apple, finely chopped
⅓ cup onion, finely chopped
3 tablespoons butter
3 tablespoons flour
1 tablespoon curry powder
1 tablespoon grated lemon rind
½ teaspoon salt
1½ cups consommé or soup stock
½ cup cream

Cook apple and onion in butter until onion becomes transparent. Blend in flour and curry powder. Stir constantly to prevent burning. Add lemon rind and salt. Stir in consommé and cream. Bring to a boil. Lower heat and stir constantly until thickened.

MEAT CURRY

1½ pounds beef or lamb, cubed
1½ cups yogurt
1 medium onion, quartered
4 slivers garlic
1 4-inch piece of ginger
½ teaspoon paprika
1 dry red or green pepper to taste
¾ teaspoon ground turmeric
1 tablespoon coriander seeds
2 tablespoons poppy seeds
1 tablespoon cumin seeds

Chili powder to taste
6 cloves
1 2-inch cinnamon stick
1 4-inch piece coconut
Salt to taste
1 cup vegetable shortening
1 large onion, thinly sliced
16 almonds, blanched and sliced
½ teaspoon saffron
¼ cup milk

Combine meat and yogurt in skillet. Cover. Simmer until half cooked — approximately ½ hour. Place quartered onion, garlic, ginger, paprika, pepper, turmeric, coriander, poppy seeds, cumin, chili powder, cloves, cinnamon, coconut and salt in food chopper using fine blade or in high-speed blender. Grind to a paste. Heat shortening in huge skillet. Add sliced onion and spice paste. Fry for 15 minutes, until onions are browned. Stir constantly. Add meat and fry lightly until meat is browned. Add almonds. Simmer meat until tender — approximately ½ hour. Crush saffron in milk. Add to meat. Cook 5 minutes more.

CHICKEN CURRY

6 to 8 chicken parts, breasts, legs
2 teaspoons ground coriander
1 teaspoon ground turmeric
4 cloves garlic, crushed
1½ teaspoons ground ginger
2 teaspoons salt
1 cup onion, chopped
1 cup tomato purée

4 tablespoons vegetable shortening
2 teaspoons sesame seeds
2 teaspoons ground cardamon
1¼ teaspoons ground cloves
1 teaspoon ground cinnamon
1 teaspoon cayenne
1 tablespoon poppy seeds, ground

Place chicken, coriander, turmeric, garlic, ginger, salt, onion and tomato purée in large skillet. Cook slowly until onions are soft. Remove from fire. Heat vegetable shortening in small skillet. Add sesame seeds, cardamon, cloves, cinnamon, cayenne and poppy seeds. Fry 3 to 4 minutes. Turn into chicken skillet. Simmer chicken until tender — approximately 1 hour.

ORANGE RICE

2 cups orange juice
1 tablespoon butter
1 tablespoon sugar
1 cup rice

2 tablespoons orange juice concentrate
2 tablespoons orange rind, grated

Bring orange juice to boil in medium saucepan. Stir in butter and sugar. Add rice; stir to mix. Cover. Simmer over low heat until rice is tender and liquid is absorbed — about 20 minutes. Add concentrate and orange rind.

RICE AND SHRIMP

4 tablespoons vegetable shortening
2 cups shrimp, cleaned and deveined
1 medium onion, thinly sliced
1 large tomato, sliced thick
4 green bell peppers, sliced in rings
Salt to taste

3 cups hot cooked rice
½ cup cooked peas
¼ cup cooked carrots, diced
1 2-egg omelet, chopped
Butter
1 medium onion, thinly sliced

Heat shortening in skillet. Fry shrimp, onion, tomato and peppers until almost dry. Add salt. Combine rice, peas, carrots and chopped omelet in mixing bowl. Spread egg and vegetable mixture over shrimp mixture. Dot with butter. Cover. Cook slowly a few minutes until butter melts. Crisp-fry onions. Garnish with onion rings.

SEASONED YOGURT

2 cups yogurt
½ cup finely chopped onion
2 tablespoons parsley or coriander leaves, chopped

¼ teaspoon chili sauce
½ teaspoon ground cumin
Salt to taste

Place all ingredients in salad bowl. Mix well. Serve.

CARROT SWEET KHEER

¼ cup almonds, coarsely chopped
6 carrots, finely grated
4 tablespoons sugar
3 cups milk

2 tablespoons heavy cream
1 teaspoon grated lemon rind
Juice of 1 lemon

Mix coarsely chopped blanched almonds (set aside some for garnish) with grated carrots, sugar and milk. Simmer, covered, very slowly over low heat until carrots absorb all milk — about 2 hours. Stir every 15 minutes. Cool. Add heavy cream and grated lemon rind. Serve sprinkled with lemon juice, topped with grated almonds.

MYRA'S FAVORITE DISHES

- SAUCISSONS D'ILE D'EAU
- JOINTS
- BAKED HARE PIE I — DILL DOUGH CRUST
- HARE PIE II
- PEASANT PHEASANT
- KOO CHI MINGE
- CUMIN COVERED COCK
- COQ AU VIN
- BREAST OF CAPON
- DAISY CHAIN
- FAIRY TALES
- LACE CURTAINS
- FRENCH KISS
- SWEET CHERRY SOUP
- FLAMING FAGGOT TROUT
- BEARDED OYSTERS
- COD PIECES
- TRICK AND TREAT
- RIBBON CLERK CASSEROLE
- QUICK TRICK
- FALLATIO ALL'ARRABIATA
- DILL DOUGH BUNS
- SCOTCH WOODCOCK
- TOAD IN THE HOLE
- GOLDEN BUCK
- CALIFORNIA QUEEN SALAD
- COCONUT BALLS
- HANNA'S BANANAS

I F what Brillat-Savarin states is true, "Tell me what you eat and I'll tell you what you are" — then I need write no further introduction for my favorite dishes. I prefer to think that my favorite dishes speak for themselves, each having its own distinct personality based upon the look, the flavor or the memory of some singular moment. Each in its own way is to be considered a work of art and like all art has taken on a life of its own, has become, as it were, Galatea to my Pygmalion (oh, that wonderful film with special favorite Leslie Howard and Wendy Hiller, later adapted into the musical *My Fair Lady* with Audrey Hepburn, who divorced Mel Ferrer and married an Italian psychiatrist, and "sexy Rexy" Harrison, once married to wonderful actress Kay Kendall).

It would be tedious to trace the emotional origins of any of these dishes back to the source. Each is meant simply to be eaten and enjoyed. I have never been more complimented than when I have served up something delicious that has been eaten with great relish. Indeed, I am always suspicious of people who do not like to eat but only pick, smell and look. They seem incomplete, incapable of taking their seat at the table of life's banquet. Eating is like sex; the better it is the more you want. In an affluent society where the essentials of survival tend to take care of themselves and the emphasis is on refinement of living, eating becomes an art in itself. Just as "sex is truly absorbing only for those who possess imagination as well as means," (*Myra Breckinridge* — Chapter 10), so it should be in twentieth-century America with cooking and eating. Still there are those who frown upon good eating and even upon sex as belonging to a decadent society. Those Americans who have escaped that "hang-up" are like their predecessors the Indians, wild but uncivilized. They could learn a lot from the French who, as we all know, have made an art out of it for centuries. The Italians, though less discriminating, love the idea of it (and let us face the fact once and for all time that one can, under the right circumstances, slyly slip almost anything past their Botticellian lips). The English, on the other hand, if they are to be taken seriously at all, must feel either guilty or upper class, while the Chinese adore it but serve too small portions. It grieves me that America, with all its enormous resources, does not lead the rest of the world in this area. Fortunately, little by little we are making progress and though the road is still far from the main highway, the bulldozers are busy and the dykes are opening up. Let us hope that perhaps some day soon, "if you wish long enough, wish strong enough" (from the song "Wishing" which was sung in *Love Affair*), our dreams will come true and we will take our rightful place amongst the nations of the world. Then maybe the words "Yankee Doodle Dandy" will finally stand for something other than just the film that starred not only James Cagney — a truly fine actor — in one of his most famous roles, but also Joan Leslie, "a star I fell hopelessly in love with while watching *Sergeant York*. But where is Joan now?" (*Myra Breckinridge* — Chapter 14)

SAUCISSONS D'ILE D'EAU
(Cassoulet)

2 pounds cooked white or navy beans
½ pound salt pork rind
¼ pound salt pork
Bouquet garni in a bag, consisting of:
  2 sprigs parsley
  6 sprigs celery tops
  2 onions, quartered
  4 cloves garlic
  2 bay leaves
  4 cloves
2 pounds garlic sausage (Italian or Polish)

2½-pound piece boneless pork loin
2½ pounds shoulder lamb
4 tablespoons shortening
2 cups chopped onions
4 cloves garlic, crushed
2 8-ounce cans tomato purée
2 cups stock
½ cup chopped parsley
½ teaspoon thyme
2 teaspoons salt
1 teaspoon pepper
2 cups bread crumbs
4 tablespoons pork fat

Put cooked beans and their water in kettle. Add pork rind, salt pork and *bouquet garni*. Simmer ½ hour. Add sausage. Meanwhile, roast pork in 350° oven about 1 hour. Bone lamb and cut into bite-size pieces. Brown lamb and bones in shortening. Add onions. Brown 5 minutes more. Add garlic, tomato purée, stock, parsley, thyme, salt and pepper. Cover. Cook 1 hour. Cut pork into bite-size pieces. Pour juices from roasted pork into lamb mixture. Drain beans. Save liquid. Remove *bouquet garni* from beans. Discard. Cut pork rind into strips. Dice salt pork. Cut sausage into thick slices. Arrange pork rind in bottom of casserole. Alternate layers of beans and meats. Pour meat juices and enough liquid from beans to cover. Top with bread crumbs and dot with pork fat. Bake in 300° to 325° oven 1½ hours. Remove cover last 30 minutes of cooking. Serves eight to ten.

JOINTS
(Braised Oxtails)

1 cup oil
6 pounds oxtails, cut in pieces at the joints
1 cup flour
1 small clove garlic, finely chopped
Rind of 1 lemon, finely chopped
2 bay leaves
Black pepper, freshly ground
2 cups red wine

1½ quarts beef stock
1 Number 2 can tomato purée
3 tablespoons salt
4 tablespoons butter
24 pearl onions
2 bunches baby carrots
1 bunch celery, cut in 1-inch pieces
2 pounds small new potatoes
1 cup fresh-cooked peas

Fry oxtails in hot oil until brown. Add flour, garlic, lemon rind, bay leaves and pepper. Add wine, beef stock, tomato purée. Bring to boil. Add salt. Let mixture simmer very slowly 2½ to 3 hours. Skim frequently.

Meanwhile, melt butter in another pan. Add onions, carrots, celery. Cook about 5 minutes, until vegetables soften. Add to ox joints. Add potatoes about ¾ hour before ox joints are cooked. Serve topped with peas.

BAKED HARE PIE I — DILL DOUGH CRUST

1 rabbit cut in pieces
Marinade: 1 tablespoon salt, pepper, 1 sliced onion, 3 sprigs parsley, pinch thyme, 1 bay leaf, crumbled, 3 tablespoons oil, ½ cup red wine

5 slices bacon, diced
12 pearl onions
½ pound mushrooms, sliced and sautéed in 2 tablespoons butter

Place rabbit in marinade for at least 6 hours — preferably overnight. Sauté bacon until golden brown. Set aside. Cook onions in bacon fat with a pinch of sugar, until golden brown. Remove onions. Add to bacon. Drain and dry each piece of rabbit. Cook in very hot bacon fat until well browned. Sprinkle with 2 tablespoons flour. Cook until flour is browned. Remove all to an earthenware casserole. Add wine and enough water to cover meat. Bring to boil. Simmer slowly 45 minutes. Add bacon, mushrooms and onions. Salt and pepper. Top with dill dough crust. Flute edges. Pierce with fork prongs. Set in moderate (350°) oven. Cook for another 30 minutes, until crust is brown.

DILL DOUGH

Make ½ box prepared biscuit mix as directed on box. Add ½ teaspoon dill seeds.

HARE PIE II

1 rabbit or	¼ teaspoon thyme
1 3-pound chicken, cut up	¼ teaspoon basil
4 tablespoons butter	¼ teaspoon Tabasco sauce
2 medium onions, sliced	1 package frozen cut corn
5 cups canned tomatoes	1 package frozen lima beans
1 cup celery, chopped	1 tablespoon cornstarch
½ cup sliced mushrooms	1 tablespoon salt
¼ teaspoon marjoram	Black pepper, freshly ground

Season rabbit or chicken with salt and pepper. Sauté in butter 10 minutes until brown. Remove chicken. Keep hot. Sauté onions in butter remaining in saucepan until lightly browned. Return chicken to pan. Add tomatoes, celery, mushrooms, herbs, Tabasco and 1 cup of water. Bring to boil. Reduce heat. Cover. Simmer 45 minutes. Add corn and lima beans. Simmer 20 minutes. Stir occasionally. Combine cornstarch with ¼ cup cold water. Add a little hot liquid from stew. Stir until smooth. Stir into stew. Simmer 5 minutes. Stir until thickened.

PEASANT PHEASANT

2 pheasants, cut up	2 tablespoons lemon juice
2 onions, quartered	6 tablespoons flour
1 celery stalk, cut up	18 pearl onions, parboiled
1 bay leaf	3 carrots, diced
2 cloves	1½ cups peas
1 teaspoon thyme	2 tablespoons pimiento strips
1 teaspoon salt	½ recipe baking powder biscuits
Black pepper, freshly ground	

Combine pheasant, onions, celery, bay leaf, cloves, thyme, salt and pepper in large saucepan with 4 cups of water. Bring to boil. Reduce heat. Cover. Simmer 45 minutes, until pheasant is tender. Remove pheasant. Strain broth. Stir in lemon juice. Add flour. Cook, stirring until broth thickens. Arrange pheasant, pearl onions, carrots, peas and pimiento in casserole. Pour in sauce. Roll biscuit dough ¼ inch thick and place over casserole. Cut slits in dough to let steam escape. Bake in hot (425°) oven 30 minutes.

KOO CHI MINGE

6 chicken breasts, boned
½ cup ground almonds
1 teaspoon salt
¼ teaspoon pepper

3 tablespoons peanut oil
¼ pound fresh mushrooms, sliced
1 cup water chestnuts, sliced
2 tablespoons soy sauce

Slice chicken into slivers. Dip in a mixture of almonds, salt and pepper. Heat oil in frying pan or skillet. Brown chicken. Add mushrooms, water chestnuts and soy sauce. Simmer at least 10 minutes.

CUMIN COVERED COCK

1 cock
1 teaspoon powdered cumin
1 cup olive oil
2 cups creamed butter
1 egg, slightly beaten

½ cup cold water
½ teaspoon salt
¼ teaspoon pepper
4 cups flour

The French sometimes use chicken. Boil cumin in olive oil for ¼ hour. Set aside. Prepare dough to cover cock: Mix butter, egg, water, salt and pepper. Mix well. Blend in flour. Place on lightly floured board. Knead with palm of hand. Work into a large sheet. Repeat kneading. Roll into ball. Wrap in waxed paper. Set aside in cool place for at least 3 hours. Prepare dressing and stuff into cavity of bird. Skewer carefully. Completely cover cock with bacon. Roll crust into 2 large rounds to cover cock. Place cock on one round. Top with other. Pinch two together all around. In center of top crust, carefully cut a round opening about 1 inch in diameter to permit steam to escape.

Wrap covered cock in waxed paper. Seal as hermetically as possible. In a fireproof earthenware dish, pour remaining cumin-flavored oil. Place cock in dish. Roast in preheated 375° oven. Roast about 1 hour, according to size of cock, allowing ¼ hour more for crust. Baste frequently. Twenty minutes before it is done, remove waxed paper to brown crust.

DRESSING

Liver of cock	3 shallots
¼ pound calf's liver	1 handful parsley
1 calf's brain, soaked in water 1 hour, parboiled 10 minutes	1 glass brandy
1 truffle	½ teaspoon salt
1 egg, beaten	¼ teaspoon pepper
	6 slices bacon

Chop chicken liver, calf's liver, calf's brain, truffle, shallots and parsley. Fry over medium heat with half cumin-flavored oil, brandy, salt and pepper. Remove from heat. Add 1 egg. Mix well.

COQ AU VIN
(Cock in Red Wine)

2 2½-pound broilers, disjointed	3 jiggers brandy
Seasoned flour	1 cup Brown Sauce (see page 322)
1 cup butter	2 cups chicken bouillon
16 button mushrooms	18 small carrots, partially cooked
2 pearl onions, chopped	12 small onions, sautéed in butter
½ teaspoon basil	18 pieces celery, 2 inches long
3 small pieces lemon peel	18 diced potatoes, sautéed in butter
2 cups good dry red wine (preferably Burgundy)	Salt and pepper

Dredge chicken in seasoned flour. Sauté until light brown on both sides. Reserve. Heat ½ cup butter in a skillet. Add mushrooms, onion, basil and lemon peel. Sauté until onion softens. Add wine. Boil 5 minutes. Add brandy. Heat. Light with match. When brandy stops burning, add Brown Sauce and chicken bouillon. Cover. Simmer until done, about 1 hour. Place chicken in casserole with carrots, onions, celery and potatoes. Return gravy to heat. Boil 5 minutes. Salt and pepper to taste. Whip remaining butter into gravy. Pour over chicken and vegetables.

JOAN COLLINS IN *Island in the Sun*

BREAST OF CAPON

6 double breasts of capon, wings attached
2 tablespoons hot Marsala wine
½ teaspoon tomato paste
1 tablespoon flour
Scant ½ cup stock

1 to 1½ cups sour cream
Salt and pepper
1 tablespoon currant jelly
1 tablespoon Parmesan cheese, grated
4 tablespoons butter

Remove meat from bone, leaving little wing bone at end. Dust lightly with flour. Brown quickly in foaming butter in skillet. Pour in wine. Remove capon. Add tomato paste and flour. Stir in stock. Stir over heat until mixture thickens. Carefully mix in sour cream. Season with salt, pepper, jelly and cheese. Return capon to pan. Cover. Cook gently 15 to 20 minutes. Remove. Arrange on ovenproof serving dish. Pour over sauce. Sprinkle with grated cheese. Dot with butter. Brown under broiler. Serve with mushrooms with wine and dill.

MUSHROOMS WITH WINE AND DILL

2 cups mushrooms
Cayenne pepper
1 tablespoon sherry
1 tablespoon finely chopped dill

Slice mushrooms fine. Sauté in very hot butter. Add salt and cayenne pepper. Cook briskly 3 to 4 minutes. Pour over sherry and finely chopped dill.

DAISY CHAIN
(Pork Sausages Flambé)

2 pounds little pork sausages
1 cup water
2 tablespoons butter

¼ cup maple syrup
⅓ cup Irish whiskey or 100 proof bourbon

Prick sausages. Cook in water over high heat 10 minutes. Pour off all water and fat. Lower heat. Add butter. Continue cooking until butter bubbles. Top with maple syrup and liquor. Heat through. Light with match. When flame dies, serve on buckwheat cakes, prepared as directed on package.

LACE CURTAINS
(Sausage Links)

18 link sausages
Beef broth
8 potatoes, peeled and sliced
Flour
Salt and pepper
2 cups milk
2 tablespoons butter

Slowly simmer sausages 10 minutes in beef broth to cover. Cut 12 sausages into small pieces. Arrange on a layer of potatoes in greased baking dish or casserole. Sprinkle with a little flour, salt and pepper to taste. Add some more sausage pieces. Repeat with another layer of potatoes, flour and sausage, ending with a layer of whole sausage on top. Pour in milk. Dot with butter. Cover with greased waxed paper to prevent browning too fast. Bake in moderate (350°) oven 1¼ to 1½ hours.

FAIRY TALES
(Pigs' Tails)

5 pigs' tails
¼ pound mushrooms, chopped
1 tablespoon butter
1 tablespoon dry sherry
2 egg yolks, slightly beaten

Trim and wash thoroughly pigs' tails. Simmer in salted water to cover until tender. Remove and drain. Save stock. Dry and set aside in warm place. Cook mushrooms in butter until they are quite brown. Cover with 1 cup of the stock and reduce stock to ½ the amount. Add sherry and the egg yolks, stirring constantly until thickened. Remove immediately from heat. Arrange hot pigs' tails on purée of peas. Serve topped with mushroom sauce.

FRENCH KISS
(Sweet-Sour Tongue)

1 medium-size fresh beef tongue	2 tablespoons vinegar
1 tablespoon salt	2 tablespoons sugar
5 slices bacon, chopped	2½ cups rolled gingersnap crumbs
3 medium-size onions, chopped	6 prunes, cooked
1 bay leaf	1 tablespoon salt
1 lemon peel	½ cup raisins
3 peppercorns	½ cup blanched almonds, sliced

In large saucepan cover beef tongue with water and 1 tablespoon salt. Simmer about 2 hours, until tender. Remove skin and all hard parts. Meanwhile: Fry bacon and onions in heavy skillet 10 minutes. Add bay leaf, lemon peel and peppercorns. Fry 5 minutes longer. Strain tongue stock. Add to mixture in skillet the strained stock (about 1 quart), the vinegar, sugar, gingersnap crumbs and prunes. Simmer 15 minutes. Taste the sauce. Add more sugar or vinegar according to taste. Add raisins and almonds. Slice tongue. Place in heatproof serving dish. Cover with sauce and reheat.

SWEET CHERRY SOUP

2 Number 2 cans pitted Bing cherries
4 cups veal stock
1 tablespoon unsweetened whipped cream

Simmer cherries with juice in saucepan for 5 minutes. Set aside twelve to use as a garnish. Blend remaining in electric blender until a thin purée. Stir into veal stock. Heat again until boiling. Serve in individual bouillon cups garnished with remaining cherries cut in pieces. Top with whipped cream.

FLAMING FAGGOT TROUT
(Trout and Fennel Flambé)

1 trout, about 3 pounds
4 cups fennel greens, washed and dried
1 cup melted butter

Pepper
Salt
3 tablespoons brandy

Wash and completely dry trout. Rub salt and pepper outside and inside. Brush with ½ cup melted butter. Butter grill. Place fish on grill. Grill under flame 25 minutes, turning twice. Brush fish with butter each time. When cooked, place on preheated fireproof dish. Pour ½ cup melted butter over fish. Cover completely with well-dried fennel greens. Pour heated brandy over all and light the fennel leaves. Serve flaming.

BEARDED OYSTERS

36 freshly opened oysters on the half shell
6 tablespoons butter
6 tablespoons raw spinach, finely minced
3 tablespoons onion, minced
3 tablespoons parsley, minced

3 tablespoons celery, minced
5 tablespoons bread crumbs
Tabasco sauce
½ teaspoon Herbsaint, absinthe or Pernod
½ teaspoon salt

Melt butter in saucepan. Add all the rest of ingredients except oysters. Cook, stirring constantly, 15 minutes or until soft. Press through sieve or food mill. Cool. Place rock salt in pie tins. Set oysters on half shell on top of rock salt. Spoon sauce on each oyster. Broil under medium heat until sauce begins to brown. Serve immediately in the pie tins.

COD PIECES

1 pound cod
Boiling oil
3 carrots, finely chopped
1 clove garlic, finely chopped
1 onion, finely chopped
2 tablespoons butter or fat
1 glass white wine

½ cup brandy
1 teaspoon tomato conserve
Pinch of paprika
½ cup water
Salt
Pepper

Cut cod in pieces. Fry in small amount of boiling oil. Drain. Brown carrots, garlic and onion in butter. Add wine, brandy, tomato conserve, paprika, water, salt and pepper. Simmer 20 minutes. Add fish. Continue cooking 15 minutes.

TRICK AND TREAT

(Broiled Lobsters)

1 onion
1 stalk celery
1 carrot
2 tablespoons vinegar
Salt

Pepper
3 live lobsters: 2 females, 1 male
Melted butter
Lemon quarters

Bring onion, celery, carrot and vinegar to a boil in salted water. Plunge live lobsters into water and cook 20 minutes. Allow to cool in water. Split in halves, removing unwanted parts. Brush with melted butter. Sprinkle with salt and charcoal-broil 15 minutes, or cook under hot broiler 15 minutes. Serve with lemon quarters and melted butter, or tomato sauce.

A more direct and simple way is to split the live lobsters, remove unwanted vein and sac, brush with melted butter, salt and pepper, and cook cut side up under preheated broiler 15 to 20 minutes, according to size. Serve hot with lemon quarters and melted butter; cold with mayonnaise.

RIBBON CLERK CASSEROLE
(Tuna Fish au Gratin)

7-ounce can tuna
¼ cup American cheese, grated
2 slices chopped onion, mixed with
    3 tablespoons butter and 1 ta-
    blespoon chopped green pepper
3 tablespoons flour
Salt and pepper to taste

1½ cups milk
½ teaspoon mustard
1 tablespoon lemon juice
1 hard-boiled egg, sliced
1 cup frozen peas
3 tablespoons bread crumbs
1 tablespoon butter

Cook onion, butter and green pepper over very low heat 5 minutes. Stir in flour, salt and pepper. Add milk gradually, stirring constantly until thick and smooth. Flake fish if necessary. Add to mixture with mustard and lemon juice. Turn into buttered baking dish. Top with peas and egg slices. Sprinkle with cheese mixed with bread crumbs. Dot with butter. Bake in moderate (350°) oven 15 minutes until well browned.

QUICK TRICK
(Oysters and Scrambled Eggs)

8 Blue Point oysters, freshly opened
4 tablespoons butter
4 eggs, well beaten
1 teaspoon anchovy paste
4 small slices warm toast, thinly
    spread with butter flavored with
    anchovy paste

Fold oysters in a napkin to absorb excess moisture. Melt butter in top pan of a chafing dish, over hot water. Add anchovy paste. Blend well with melted butter. Scramble eggs into the mixture. When slightly set, push against sides of pan to make a space in center. Add oysters. When just heated and edges curl slightly, cover with cooked scrambled eggs. Add pepper to taste — the anchovy paste is already salted. Serve on anchovy buttered toast.

FALLATIO ALL'ARRABIATA

6 tablespoons fresh Italian olive oil
1 medium-size onion, thinly sliced
½ pound lean bacon, coarsely chopped
¼ pound sausage meat
1 fresh tomato, chopped
3 or 4 cloves garlic, halved
2 or 3 dried Italian pepperoni torn in half

2 Number 2 cans Italian tomatoes
Salt to taste
10 peppercorns
2 bay leaves
1½ pounds Italian spaghetti
2 tablespoons coarse salt
½ cup Parmesan cheese, freshly grated

Chop onion, bacon, sausage and tomato. Sauté onion in olive oil until golden brown. Add bacon. When slightly crisp, add sausages. Fry until firm. Add tomato, garlic, pepperoni, canned tomatoes, salt, peppercorns and bay leaves. Simmer 1 to 1½ hours.

Cook spaghetti in 4 quarts boiling water. Add 2 tablespoons of olive oil and 2 tablespoons coarse salt. Boil until *al dente* — tender but still firm. Drain in colander. Put in large serving bowl. Pour sauce over all. Mix well. Top with cheese. Serve with sauceboat of extra sauce and more grated cheese.

DILL DOUGH BUNS

2 cups sifted flour
1 tablespoon double-acting baking powder
1 teaspoon salt
½ cup shortening
⅔ cup milk
½ teaspoon dried dill seed

Sift flour with baking powder and salt. Blend in shortening until mixture resembles coarse meal. Add milk and dill. Stir until soft dough is formed. Knead gently on lightly floured board 30 seconds. Roll or pat dough ½ inch thick. Cut into 12 biscuits. Bake on a baking sheet in hot (425°) oven 15 minutes.

DOROTHY LAMOUR IN *Spawn of the North*

SCOTCH WOODCOCK

12 eggs, lightly beaten
Salt
Black pepper, freshly ground
3 tablespoons butter

½ cup dry sherry
6 slices toast
6 anchovy fillets, chopped

Beat eggs with salt and pepper until foamy. Cook in butter. Stir slowly over low heat until eggs begin to set. Stir in sherry. Continue cooking until done. Serve eggs on top of toast. Sprinkle with anchovy fillets.

TOAD IN THE HOLE

For each person:
1 egg
1 slice bread
3 tablespoons butter

Cut a circle out of center of the bread. Fry bread in butter until brown and crisp on one side. Turn. Break egg into the circle. Fry over low heat about 5 minutes or until the egg is cooked.

GOLDEN BUCK

4½ cups Cheddar cheese, grated
1½ teaspoons English mustard
1½ teaspoons cornstarch
1½ tablespoons Worcestershire

1 cup beer
Salt to taste
6 poached eggs

Mix cheese, mustard and cornstarch in heavy casserole. Add Worcestershire, beer and salt to taste. Stir over medium heat. Bring to boil. Stir constantly. When cheese is melted and smooth, serve on English muffins. Top each with a poached egg.

CALIFORNIA QUEEN SALAD

Shredded lettuce
6 stewed pear halves
Bits of ripe olives
Pimiento strips
1½ cups cottage cheese mixed with
½ cup cream cheese

Avocado balls
Sliced stuffed olives
Juice of 1 lemon
2 lemons, cut in quarters

Place a mound of finely shredded lettuce on chilled salad plate. Arrange pears spoke-like in a circle. Place a scoop of cottage and cream cheese, mixed, in center. Top with avocado balls and sliced olives. Garnish with olive bits and pimiento strips. Serve with lemon juice and slices.

COCONUT BALLS
(Ice Cream Balls in Coconut)

Roll balls of chocolate ice cream in freshly grated coconut early in the day. Keep them in freezer until serving time.

HANNA'S BANANAS

12 bananas, ripe but firm — peeled
¼ cup dark brown sugar
¼ cup white sugar
4 tablespoons butter
Juice of 1 lemon

For Sauce:
1½ to 1¾ cups water
½ cup white sugar
½ cup muscat seedless raisins
3 tablespoons cornstarch
1 tablespoon butter
Nutmeg
1 tablespoon lemon juice

Butter a 9 by 12 inch baking dish. Line with whole bananas. Sprinkle with brown sugar, then with white sugar. Dot with butter. Pour over lemon juice. Bake in moderate (350°) oven until brown — about 25 minutes.

Meanwhile prepare sauce: Boil water, sugar and raisins for five minutes. Add cornstarch, dissolved in 2 tablespoons cold water. Boil again to thicken. Add butter, a few grains nutmeg and the lemon juice.

Set baked bananas under broiler for about five minutes. Remove. Cover with boiling sauce. Cook in oven until bubbly. These can be served with either whipped cream or heavy sweet cream.

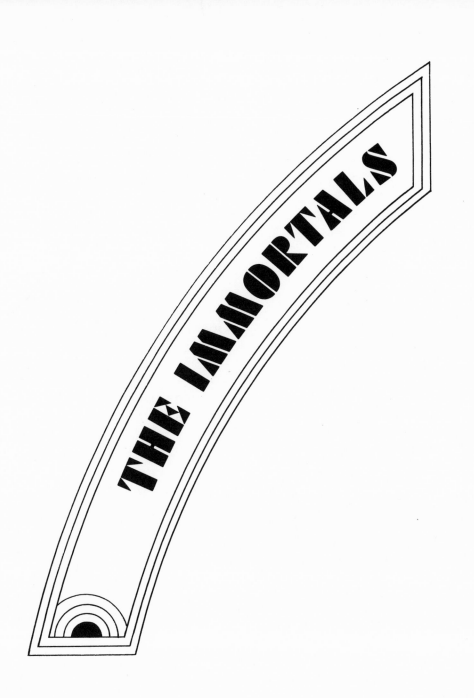

- BOUILLABAISSE
- GAZPACHO
- MANHATTAN CLAM CHOWDER
- FRENCH ONION SOUP
- MOULES MARINIÈRE
- COLD SALMON MOUSSE
- LOBSTER THERMIDOR
- LOBSTER BASQUE STYLE
- BAKED CHERRYSTONES
- ABALONE STEAKS
- SEAFOOD SALAD
- POLYNESIAN FISH
- SHAD ROE
- CAESAR SALAD
- CHICKEN-FILLED AVOCADO
- GREEN GODDESS SALAD
- CHICKEN SHERRY CREAM
- NEW ORLEANS CHICKEN AND CRAB GUMBO
- COQ AU VIN BLANC
- SOUTHERN FRIED CHICKEN
- OYSTER-STUFFED CHICKEN
- BARBECUED CHICKEN
- CHICKEN MARENGO
- CHICKEN À L'ORANGE
- PÂTÉ BRANDY STUFFING
- ROAST TURKEY IN FOIL
- ROAST STUFFED GOOSE AND BAKED APPLES
- DUCK IN PORT WINE
- BEEF BOURGUIGNON
- RAGOUT OF BEEF
- ROAST FILLET OF BEEF
- SAUERBRATEN
- VEAL STEW HOME STYLE
- HUNGARIAN GOULASH
- VEAL AND PORK MEAT LOAF
- CROWN ROAST OF PORK
- MILK-BAKED HAM STEAK
- BAKED PORK CHOPS FLORENTINE
- KIDNEYS IN MUSTARD SAUCE
- SMOKED TONGUE AND KUMQUAT MOUSSE
- LAMB WITH EGGPLANT PURÉE
- BREADED LAMB CHOPS
- SHASHLIK
- MILK-FED LEG OF LAMB
- GAUCHO LAMB
- PHEASANT IN CREAM
- PHEASANT WITH WEINKRAUT
- ROAST SADDLE OF YOUNG BOAR
- POTATOES STUFFED WITH MUSH-ROOMS
- SPINACH SOUFFLÉ
- FRESH FRUIT GELATIN
- BAKED PINEAPPLE
- CHOCOLATE SOUFFLÉ WITH CRÈME DE CACAO
- RUDOLPH VALENTINO: Italian Food

We deal in *myths*. At any given moment the world requires one full-bodied Aphrodite (Jean Harlow), one dark siren of flawless beauty (Hedy Lamarr), one powerful inarticulate brute of a man (John Wayne), one smooth debonair charmer (Melvyn Douglas), one world-weary corrupt lover past his prime (Humphrey Bogart), one eternal good-sex woman-wife (Myrna Loy), one wide-eyed chicken boy (Lon McAllister), one gentle girl singer (Susanna Foster), one winning stud (Clark Gable), one losing stud outside the law (James Cagney), and so on. Olympus supports many gods and goddesses and they are truly eternal, since whenever one fades or falls another promptly takes his place, for the race requires that the pantheon be always filled.
— *Myra Breckinridge*, CHAPTER 23

THESE gods and goddesses, immortal, have in their time broken my heart, made my sides split laughing, given me runny noses and countless numbers of cracked chafed lips. How can I show my appreciation? I feel such veneration and gratitude to these immortals who have made our lives happier, hornier and better — and in the process have kept alive "what began that day in the theatre of Dionysos when Aeschylus first spoke to the Athenians" (*Myra Breckinridge* — Chapter 9). Silly words are wanting, and even though these ensuing recipes have been chosen and dedicated to these immortals (for those self-same qualities of timelessness and simplicity that all immortals have) there can be no form of adulation adequate enough for those who have changed from man to myth. I cannot say more.

BOUILLABAISSE

¼ cup carrot, chopped
1 cup onion, chopped
1 clove garlic, minced
½ cup olive oil
3 pounds frozen fish fillets,
    cut in pieces
2½ cups canned tomatoes
1 bay leaf, crumbled
6 frozen lobster tails
1 cup frozen shrimps

1 cup frozen crab meat
1 can whole mussels
1½ cups dry white wine
1 tablespoon lemon juice
¼ cup parsley, chopped
½ cup pimiento, diced
½ teaspoon saffron
Salt
Freshly ground black pepper

Sauté carrot, onion and garlic in olive oil ten minutes. Add fish fillets, tomatoes, bay leaf and 2 quarts of water. Bring to boil. Reduce heat. Simmer 20 minutes. Add lobster tails, shells split down middle, shrimp, crab, mussels and remaining ingredients. Simmer 30 minutes.

GAZPACHO

4 cups tomatoes, diced
1½ cups green pepper, chopped
¾ cup onion, chopped
1 clove garlic, minced
2 cups beef bouillon
½ cup lemon juice

¼ cup olive oil
1 tablespoon paprika
½ cup cucumber, diced
1 tablespoon salt
Freshly ground black pepper

Combine all ingredients, setting aside 1 tablespoon each of tomato, green pepper, cucumber, and toasted croutons for garnishing. Blend ingredients in electric blender. Chill for at least 2 hours before serving. Garnish with diced tomato, green pepper, cucumber and toasted croutons.

MANHATTAN CLAM CHOWDER

1 dozen large clams
6 strips bacon, cut in small pieces
1 large onion, chopped
1 leek, finely sliced
3 potatoes, cut in cubes
4 tomatoes, peeled and chopped
2 stalks celery, chopped
1 green pepper, chopped

1 bay leaf
½ teaspoon thyme
5 cups water
Clam liquor
Salt
Pepper
½ teaspoon caraway seed

Steam clams until shells open. Add no water. Reserve liquor from clams. Cut clams into small pieces. Sauté bacon in a soup kettle. Add onion and leek. Cook until vegetables are lightly browned. Add potatoes, tomatoes, celery, green pepper, bay leaf, thyme, water and liquor from clams. Season with salt and pepper to taste.

Cover. Bring mixture to a boil. Reduce heat. Simmer 30 minutes until vegetables are tender. Add clams and caraway seed. Continue to cook 5 minutes. Serve very hot, with chowder biscuits.

FRENCH ONION SOUP

12 chopped onions
3 tablespoons olive oil
4 tablespoons butter
3 tablespoons flour
2½ quarts chicken bouillon
¼ teaspoon Worcestershire sauce

¼ teaspoon Tabasco sauce
Salt
Freshly ground black pepper
6 1-inch slices French bread
1 cup grated Swiss or Parmesan cheese

Sauté onions in oil and butter in a large saucepan, slowly, for 15 minutes or until softened but not brown. Blend in flour. Add bouillon, Worcestershire, Tabasco, pepper and salt. Bring to boil, reduce heat, cover and simmer for 2 hours. Toast French bread in a moderate oven (350°) until brown on both sides. Sprinkle each slice with cheese. Broil under low heat until cheese is browned. Serve toast with the soup.

MOULES MARINIÈRE
(Stewed Mussels)

5 quarts mussels
¾ cup dry white wine
1 teaspoon shallots or green onions, chopped
1 teaspoon onion, chopped

1 teaspoon parsley, chopped
Freshly ground black pepper
3 teaspoons heavy cream
2½ tablespoons butter blended with 2 teaspoons flour

Scrub mussels thoroughly. Place in kettle with wine and chopped vegetables. Add freshly ground pepper to taste. Cover tightly and cook over high heat until all the shells are open (about 5 minutes). Drain and save the liquid. Put mussels in a serving dish. Keep warm.

Strain liquid. Pour liquid very slowly into a saucepan. Reduce over high heat to one-third its original volume. Add cream. Blend butter with flour. Add to sauce. Cook until thickened. Pour over the mussels.

COLD SALMON MOUSSE

1 salmon, about ¾ pound
1 onion
1 carrot
1 bay leaf
¼ cup white wine
¾ cup butter
2 tablespoons sherry

2 tablespoons cream

For Béchamel Sauce:
3 tablespoons butter
3 tablespoons flour
1 cup milk
Salt and pepper

Prepare Béchamel Sauce: Melt 3 tablespoons butter in a pan. Add 3 tablespoons flour. Stir until smooth. Add 1 cup milk. Season. Stir over heat until boiling. Remove and let cool.

Place salmon, onion, carrot, bay leaf, wine and a little water in a pan. Boil slowly. Simmer 20 minutes. Cool in the stock. Skin and bone salmon. Pound thoroughly with ¾ cup creamed butter and the Béchamel Sauce. When well pounded, add sherry and cream. Fill a soufflé dish with mixture. Spread smooth. Remove to a cool place.

JOHN BARRYMORE AND MARY ASTOR IN *Don Juan*

LOBSTER THERMIDOR

2 1¼-pound live lobsters
4 tablespoons oil
3 tablespoons butter
1 medium-size onion, finely chopped
½ cup dry white wine
2 tablespoons flour
Salt
Cayenne pepper
¾ cup milk
¼ cup cream
Pinch dry mustard
Pinch paprika
Handful grated Parmesan cheese

Wash lobsters well in cold water. Split in half, starting from the little cross in the center of the head. Remove small bag from behind eyes. Cook, covered, split side down in heated oil. Cook slowly 12 minutes. Remove carefully. Reserve stock. Take lobster meat from shells and cut in chunks. Place shells on hot serving dish and keep warm. Kill by inserting a sharp knife between the body and shell at the tail to sever the spinal cord.

Melt 2 tablespoons butter in pan. Add onion. Cook until soft without browning. Add wine. Cook slowly until wine has evaporated. In another pan heat 1 tablespoon butter. Stir in flour, salt and cayenne pepper. Stir until smooth. Add milk. Stir over heat until mixture comes to a boil. Add with cream, mustard, paprika and 2 tablespoons cheese to onion mixture. Reduce to thick, creamy consistency by adding a little of the lobster stock. Mix with lobster meat. Fill shells with mixture. Sprinkle well with grated cheese. Dot with remaining butter. Brown quickly under broiler and serve.

LOBSTER BASQUE STYLE

3 small lobsters, about 1 pound each
4 tablespoons butter
1 large carrot, thinly sliced
2 medium-size onions
1 leek
1 tablespoon flour
1 cup white wine, heated
1 cup bouillon, heated
½ cup parsley
½ cup fennel tops
½ teaspoon basil, diced
4 cloves garlic, crushed
Cayenne
1 pinch saffron
4 tablespoons tomato purée
Salt
Pepper

Cook lobsters in salted boiling water about 18 to 20 minutes. Meanwhile: Melt butter in saucepan with carrot, onions (stick a clove in each) and the white of the leek. When well coated with butter, sprinkle with flour. Mix well. Slowly add wine, bouillon, parsley, fennel, basil, garlic, cayenne, saffron, tomato purée, salt and pepper. Cover. Cook slowly 1 hour. Cut lobsters lengthwise. Remove meat and place in a heated casserole. Remove meat from claws and add to casserole. You may strain the sauce, if desired. Pour sauce over lobster meat and serve in the casserole.

BAKED CHERRYSTONES

36 cherrystone clams on the half shell	¼ cup green pepper, diced
	½ cup pimiento, diced
3 slices bacon, diced	1 teaspoon onion, minced

Set clams in shells on a bed of rock salt. Arrange in pie tins. Mix bacon, green pepper, pimiento, onions, and sprinkle on clams. Bake in hot (400°) oven 15 minutes until bacon is brown.

ABALONE STEAKS

2 pounds abalone steaks	2 teaspoons parsley, minced
2 cups flour	Juice of lemon
1½ cups milk mixed with 2 beaten eggs	Beurre Amandine (¾ cup slivered almonds browned in butter)
½ pound butter	

Dip abalone steaks in flour, then in egg batter, and again in flour. Fry in butter in a heavy skillet. Fry quickly, about 3 minutes on each side. Turn just once. Remove from pan. Arrange on hot plate. Top with parsley. Sprinkle with lemon juice. Cover with almonds.

SEAFOOD SALAD

1½ cups cooked crab meat	Mixed greens
1 cup cooked lobster meat	6 ripe olives, halved
1½ cups cooked shrimp	6 strips pimiento
3 tomatoes, sliced	Salad dressing

CLARA BOW

Arrange crab, lobster, shrimp and tomatoes on bed of mixed greens. Garnish with olives and pimiento. To serve, toss with classic French Dressing (see page 323).

POLYNESIAN FISH

3 pounds halibut, cut ¾ inch thick
⅓ cup lime juice
¼ cup melted butter
½ teaspoon salt
¼ teaspoon freshly ground pepper

Generous pinch of marjoram
½ can frozen cream of shrimp soup
½ cup sour cream
3 or 4 scallions, with tops, sliced thin
12 tiny shrimp

Wash, dry and cut fish into 6 pieces. Place in ovenproof shallow baking dish. Pour lime juice over the top and allow to soak a few minutes on each side. Drain off juice. Pour butter over fish and sprinkle with seasonings. Broil about 10 minutes. Baste once. Remove from heat, baste again. Set aside to cool slightly. Mix soup and sour cream and spoon on top of each piece of fish. (All this may be prepared ahead). When ready, bake 30 minutes in moderately slow (325°) oven. Serve in baking dish garnished with scallions and shrimp.

SHAD ROE

6 sets fresh shad roe
3 tablespoons butter
1 teaspoon fresh pepper
1 teaspoon dill, chopped fine

2 cups white wine
1 bay leaf, crushed
8 rashers bacon
8 slices lemon, very thin

Wash shad roe in softly running cold water. Lay roe in buttered baking dish. Dot with butter. Sprinkle with freshly ground pepper and dill. Pour in white wine. Add bay leaf. Bake in preheated, hot (450°) oven 30 minutes. Baste frequently. Meanwhile, fry bacon over low heat until crisp. Drain. Crumble. When roe is cooked, transfer to hot platter. Pour wine over the roe and top with crumbled bacon.

CAESAR SALAD

Salt to taste
Freshly ground black pepper to taste
1 clove garlic, crushed
1 teaspoon mustard
1½ tablespoons lemon juice
3½ tablespoons olive oil
2 bunches romaine lettuce, washed
    and dried

2 tablespoons grated Parmesan
    cheese
1 can anchovies, drained
2 eggs boiled for 1 minute
1 cup toasted croutons

Sprinkle salt and pepper in bottom of a wooden salad bowl. Add garlic, mustard and lemon juice. Mix until salt dissolves. Add olive oil. Stir until well blended.

Wash romaine well and dry leaves. Tear lettuce leaves into bite-sized pieces. Add to salad bowl. Add Parmesan and anchovies. Break eggs over salad. Sprinkle with croutons. Mix thoroughly.

CHICKEN-FILLED AVOCADO

4 avocados, peeled
4 teaspoons lemon juice
½ cup mayonnaise
2 cups cooked chicken, diced
1 cup white grapes, seeded or seed-
    less

½ cup almonds
½ teaspoon salt
Purple grapes

Cut avocados in half lengthwise. Remove seeds. Scoop out a teaspoonful of pulp from center of each avocado. Mash with 1½ teaspoons lemon juice. Add mayonnaise. Sprinkle 1½ teaspoons lemon juice over avocado halves. Combine chicken, white grapes, almonds, salt, remaining lemon juice and ¾ of mayonnaise mixture. Fill avocado halves. Place on lettuce leaves. Top with remaining mayonnaise mixture. Garnish with purple grapes.

GREEN GODDESS SALAD

1 pound raw spinach, torn in pieces
2 cups Green Goddess Salad Dressing
2 cups bread croutons

Toss well-washed spinach in a medium-sized salad bowl with Green Goddess Salad Dressing. Just before serving, mix in croutons.

GREEN GODDESS SALAD DRESSING

1 tablespoon lemon juice	2 tablespoons vinegar
½ cup heavy cream	½ teaspoon onion juice
1 cup mayonnaise	¼ cup onion, finely chopped
2 tablespoons tarragon vinegar	⅓ cup parsley, finely chopped
2 tablespoons garlic vinegar	

Add lemon juice to cream. Mix with remaining ingredients.

CHICKEN SHERRY CREAM

1 10½-ounce can cream of chicken soup	½ cup whipping cream
1 cup cooked chicken, cut into cubes	¾ cup sherry
1 13-ounce can madrilène	Chopped chives

Blend chicken soup with chicken in electric blender until finely chopped. Heat madrilène in small saucepan just until boiling. Add to chicken mixture. Blend well in electric blender. Add cream and sherry. Blend thoroughly. Serve sprinkled with chopped chives.

NEW ORLEANS CHICKEN AND CRAB GUMBO

¼ cup butter	1 bay leaf
½ cup onion, chopped	½ teaspoon basil
⅓ cup green peppers, chopped	¼ teaspoon thyme
½ cup lean raw ham, cut in chunks	¼ cup parsley, minced
1 cup cooked chicken, diced	Salt and cayenne pepper to taste
1 cup raw okra, sliced	½ cup bourbon
1 pint tomato juice	⅓ teaspoon gumbo filé (optional)
1 cup raw shelled deveined shrimp	Steamed rice
1 pound crab meat	
1 quart boiling water or chicken stock	

Brown onion, pepper, ham, chicken and okra in melted butter. Add tomato juice, shrimp, crab meat, boiling water or stock, bay leaf, basil, thyme and parsley. Season to taste with salt and cayenne. Bring to boil.

JEAN HARLOW

Lower heat. Simmer in covered pan 20 minutes. Add bourbon. Cook 5 minutes. Remove from heat. Stir in filé powder, if desired. Serve with rice.

NOTE: Never reheat gumbo after filé powder has been added.

COQ AU VIN BLANC
(Chicken in White Wine)

1 young chicken
3 tablespoons butter
¾ cup bacon, diced
6 pearl onions
4 shallots, thinly sliced
1 medium-sized carrot, thinly sliced

Salt and pepper
2 garlic cloves, crushed
1 jigger brandy
1 tablespoon flour
1 cup fresh mushrooms, sliced
1 cup dry white wine

Cut chicken in serving pieces. In heavy skillet brown bacon, onions, shallots and carrot in butter. Remove from skillet. Set aside. Add chicken to skillet. Brown over high heat. Add salt, pepper and garlic. Heat brandy. Light and pour into skillet. Sprinkle with flour. Stir with wooden spoon a few minutes. Add mushrooms and white wine. Add bacon and vegetables. Cook uncovered ¾ hour, until done.

SOUTHERN FRIED CHICKEN

2 3-pound frying chickens, disjointed
2 eggs
1 cup milk
2 teaspoons salt

½ teaspoon pepper
1 cup flour
Shortening for deep fat frying

Clean chickens carefully. Beat eggs well. Add milk, salt and pepper. Mix chicken pieces in the mixture. Be sure each piece is coated. Allow to stand 10 minutes in the mixture. Remove chicken. Roll in flour. Heat shortening to 360°. Place a few pieces of chicken at a time in a frying basket. Lower into fat. Fry until golden brown on all sides. As pieces are removed, keep them warm until all of the chicken is fried. Serve with a cream gravy.

CREAM GRAVY
2 tablespoons fat in which the chicken was fried
1 tablespoon flour
1 cup light cream, scalded

Place fat in a saucepan. Stir in flour until smooth. Gradually add scalded cream. Stir constantly until boiling. Correct seasoning. Spoon over chicken pieces.

OYSTER-STUFFED CHICKEN

1 pint oysters	3 tablespoons onion, finely chopped
3 broiler chickens, split in half	1 garlic clove, crushed
Butter	1 cup bread crumbs
2 tablespoons green pepper, chopped	¼ teaspoon cayenne pepper
4 tablespoons celery, chopped	1 teaspoon salt
3 tablespoons parsley, chopped	Black pepper, freshly ground
⅛ teaspoon powdered sage	Cranberry or loganberry preserve

Drain and chop oysters. Reserve liquor. Sauté oysters with green pepper, celery, parsley, sage, onion and garlic 10 minutes. Mix in 1 cup bread crumbs, teaspoon salt, black pepper and ½ cup oyster liquor. Meanwhile: Place chickens in shallow baking pan skin side up. Dot with butter. Add ½ cup water to pan. Bake in moderate (375°) oven 30 minutes, until brown. Remove chicken from oven. Turn skin side down. Fill cavities with oyster stuffing. Top with more bread crumbs and melted butter. Bake 20 minutes, until crumbs are golden brown.

Serve with cranberry or loganberry preserve.

BARBECUED CHICKEN

3 2-pound chickens, cut up	2 tablespoons parsley, chopped
½ cup dry white wine	¼ teaspoon oregano
1 garlic clove, crushed	Tomato-wine sauce (2 parts tomato
½ cup oil	purée, 1 part white wine)
1 teaspoon chives, chopped	

Marinate chicken at room temperature 1 hour in wine, garlic, oil, chives, parsley and oregano. Turn chicken occasionally. Broil 30 minutes. Baste with tomato-wine sauce. Turn frequently until done.

GRETA GARBO

CHICKEN MARENGO

2½ pounds broilers, cut up
Flour
Salt and pepper
8 tablespoons olive oil
12 mushrooms, sliced
1 small onion, chopped fine

1 cup white wine
4 medium-sized tomatoes, diced
12 pitted green olives, sliced
1 cup Brown Sauce
½ teaspoon basil
4 tablespoons butter

Roll chicken in flour with salt and pepper. Brown in hot oil on both sides. Add mushrooms and onions. Sauté a few minutes. Add wine. Cover. Add tomatoes, olives, Brown Sauce and basil. Cover. Simmer 15 minutes. Should sauce become too thick, add chicken broth. Just before serving, add butter. Serve with rice.

BROWN SAUCE

1 heaping tablespoon butter
½ heaping tablespoon flour
1 cup consommé, heated

1 tablespoon tomato purée
Salt
Pepper

Add flour to melted butter. Stir well until flour is light brown. Add consommé. Stir well to dissolve all lumps. Add tomato purée, salt and pepper. Simmer slowly 10 minutes and strain.

CHICKEN À L'ORANGE

3 broiler chickens, halved
1 teaspoon salt
Black pepper, freshly ground
4 tablespoons butter, melted
4 tablespoons lime juice
1 cup red currant jelly
1 6-ounce can frozen concentrated orange juice

1 teaspoon dry mustard
⅓ cup dry sherry
⅛ teaspoon ground ginger
¼ teaspoon Tabasco sauce
Grated rind of 1 orange

Rub chicken with salt and pepper. Broil under medium heat 1 hour. Turn once. Baste frequently with mixed butter and lime juice. Meanwhile: Mix jelly, orange juice, mustard, sherry, ginger and Tabasco sauce. Simmer until smooth. Stir constantly. Spoon over chicken. Garnish with orange rind. Serve remainder in sauce boat.

PÂTÉ BRANDY STUFFING

4 slices stale bread
White wine
6 strips bacon
½ cup butter
1 pound chicken livers cut in
    small pieces
Salt and pepper
¼ cup onion, finely chopped
½ cup celery, coarsely chopped
2 tablespoons parsley, minced

¼ cup cooked or canned
    mushroom pieces
¼ teaspoon basil
½ teaspoon thyme
⅛ teaspoon marjoram
⅛ teaspoon rosemary
½ cup brandy
1 egg, well beaten
Salt and pepper to taste

Soak bread in wine for 30 minutes. Sauté bacon. Remove strips from pan. Squeeze wine from bread and retain ¼ cup wine. Melt butter until bubbly (360°). Put aside. Sprinkle livers with salt and pepper and sauté for 4 minutes in bacon fat. Add onion, celery, parsley and mushrooms. Cook until onion is clear, mashing the livers while they are cooking. Reduce heat. Add bread, ¼ cup wine reserved, basil, thyme, marjoram, rosemary and crumbled bacon strips. Cook, stirring and mashing with fork, until there are no lumps of bread in mixture. When bread begins to brown, stir in brandy and continue cooking over low heat, stirring constantly, until brandy is blended with rest of mixture. Remove from heat and, when cool, blend in softened butter and egg, and season to taste with salt and pepper. Makes about 2½ quarts stuffing.

Good for chicken or turkey.

ROAST TURKEY IN FOIL

1 turkey
Salt
Water

Softened butter
Stuffing

Rub turkey inside and out with salt. Fill neck and body with stuffing. Fasten cavities with poultry pins. Lace with cord. Fasten legs to sides of bird. Wrap in tight covering of aluminum foil. Put breast side down in roasting pan for first hour of roasting. Turn breast side up for rest of the time. Have a small quantity of water in bottom of roasting pan at all times. Allow 22 minutes a pound in a moderate (350°) oven. Test by inserting skewer into fleshy part of thigh. If skewer goes in easily and juice that flows out is clear and not pink, the bird is cooked. Remove foil about ½ hour before finished and brush well with softened butter.

ROAST STUFFED GOOSE AND BAKED APPLES

8-pound goose, with giblets	Dash of pepper
2 quarts bread crumbs	Additional salt
2 onions, chopped	6 apples
2 stalks celery, chopped	¼ cup brown sugar
2 tablespoons butter	3 cooked, mashed and seasoned
1 teaspoon sage	sweet potatoes
2 teaspoons salt	

Cook giblets in water until tender. Chop and mix with bread crumbs, onions, celery, butter, sage, salt and pepper. Reserve for stuffing. Before stuffing goose, prick skin into fat layer around legs and wings. Heat in preheated oven (375°) 15 minutes. Drain off fat. Repeat twice. Rub inside of goose with salt. Stuff with giblet mixture. Truss with picks.

Roast uncovered in slow oven (325°) until tender — about 25 minutes per pound.

Wash and core apples; sprinkle with brown sugar. Fill with seasoned sweet potatoes. Add to roasting pan with goose 1 hour before goose is cooked.

DUCK IN PORT WINE

1 duck
24 Kadota figs
1 bottle port wine
1 cup veal bouillon

Marinate figs in port wine, in sealed wide-mouthed jar, for about 36 hours. On the day of the dinner, roast the duck in preheated 450° oven. After 15 minutes, baste with heated port wine (in which the figs have been marinating). Baste every 15 minutes. Turn duck on each side to brown. After 35 minutes, set figs around duck and continue basting with hot veal bouillon for another 25 minutes or until duck is tender.

CLARK GABLE

BEEF BOURGUIGNON

4½ pounds beef sirloin, cut in 1-inch
　　cubes
¾ cup butter
3 cups mushroom caps, sliced

1½ cups onions, chopped
2 tablespoons flour
3 cups red wine, preferably
　　Burgundy

Melt 5 tablespoons butter in deep casserole. Add beef cubes. Cover. Braise in hot oven (400°) for 20 minutes. Meanwhile, sauté mushrooms and onions in remaining butter. Stir in flour. Add Burgundy and mix well. Pour over beef. Cover. Return to oven for 30 minutes.

RAGOUT OF BEEF

2½ pounds top round of beef
　　cut in chunks
Claret
Salt and pepper
Flour
⅓ cup butter
Flour
1½ cups beef bouillon
Marinade
2 carrots, scraped and sliced
2 tablespoons onion, chopped

¼ cup parsley, minced
¼ cup celery, minced
⅓ cup canned mushrooms
Salt and pepper
⅛ teaspoon thyme
⅛ teaspoon rosemary
⅛ teaspoon basil
⅛ teaspoon tarragon
2 tablespoons port
2 teaspoons champagne cognac

Marinate meat in claret to cover. Refrigerate at least 4 hours. Drain and dry beef. Reserve marinade. Sprinkle meat with salt and pepper. Dredge with flour. Brown meat in skillet on all sides in butter. Place meat in deep heavy saucepan. Strain grease and return to skillet. Heat until bubbly. Stir in 1 tablespoon flour. Cook over medium heat until brown and smooth. Remove from heat. Add bouillon and marinade. Bring to boil. Stir constantly. Pour over meat. Add carrots, onion, parsley, celery and mushrooms. Cover. Cook over low heat 15 minutes. Season with salt and pepper. Add thyme, rosemary, basil and tarragon. Cover. Simmer slowly until meat is tender (about 45 minutes). Add port and cognac. Heat through.

ROAST FILET OF BEEF

2 pounds filet of beef	2 black truffles, thinly sliced
24 button onions	12 tiny whole tomatoes
2 tablespoons butter	

Roast filet 10 minutes in hot (400°) oven (rare). Season onions with salt and pepper. Cook in butter in a covered pan. Add truffles. Add tomatoes. Warm through. Place beef on serving platter. Place onions and tomato around fillet and top with truffles. Add juice from roasting pan.

SAUERBRATEN

4 pounds bottom or top round	¼ cup bacon grease
1½ teaspoon salt	2 tablespoons sifted flour
¾ teaspoon black pepper	8 small gingersnaps, crushed
1 cup vinegar	Salt and pepper to taste
4/5 quart Burgundy wine	Sugar to taste (1½ to 2½ table-
Water	spoons)
2 small bay leaves	¼ cup red Burgundy wine
6 cloves	Water or sugar or vinegar to taste, if
¾ cup onion, chopped	needed
1 tablespoon dehydrated parsley	⅔ cup sour cream

Sprinkle meat with salt and black pepper. Place in earthenware casserole. Add vinegar, wine, water to cover, bay leaves, cloves, onion and parsley. Cover casserole. Set in refrigerator for 48 hours. Turn now and then. Remove meat from marinade. Strain marinade. Reserve 2 cups. Brown meat on all sides in skillet in hot bacon grease. Place meat in roasting pan. Stir flour into bubbling grease in skillet. Cook, constantly stirring, until brown. Add marinade. Stir until smooth. Add gingersnaps, salt, pepper and sugar. Stir until thick and smooth. Pour over roast. Bake in 350° oven. Baste every 30 minutes. Allow 28 minutes per pound. Thirty minutes before done, pour wine over meat. Blend with gravy and adjust sweet-sour taste. Boil gravy. Stir in sour cream just before serving. Serve on heated platter.

VEAL STEW HOME STYLE

4 tablespoons fat
1¾ pounds boneless veal, cubed
½ cup cider vinegar
½ cup boiling water
1 cup carrots, diced
12 small white onions

½ cup freshly shelled peas
1 bay leaf
1 sprig thyme
6 sprigs fresh parsley
Salt
Pepper

Brown veal in fat in a heavy pot. Brown well on all sides. Stir constantly. Stir in vinegar and water. Bring to boil. Add carrots, onions, peas, bay leaf, thyme and parsley. Salt and pepper to taste. Simmer, covered, very slowly 40 minutes.

HUNGARIAN GOULASH

1½ pounds veal from leg, cut in
    large squares
2 tablespoons butter
2 onions, sliced
2 carrots, sliced
1 celery stalk
1 garlic clove, crushed
1 tablespoon paprika

1 green pepper, shredded
1 red pepper, shredded
1 tablespoon tomato paste
1 tablespoon flour
2 cups stock
Salt and pepper
1 bay leaf, crushed
1 cup sour cream

Brown veal very quickly in hot butter. Remove the meat. Cook onions, carrots, celery and garlic in same pan slowly 5 to 6 minutes. Add paprika. Cook another 5 minutes. Add half the peppers. Stir in tomato paste, flour and stock. Stir until boiling. Add salt, pepper, veal and bay leaf. Cover. Slowly cook until meat is quite tender. Remove to a casserole. Strain stock and return to the pan with remaining peppers. Reduce to thick consistency and pour over veal. Just before serving add sour cream.

JOAN CRAWFORD IN *Rain*

VEAL AND PORK MEAT LOAF

¾ pound veal, finely ground
¾ pound lean pork, finely ground
1 cup mushrooms, chopped
¼ cup fresh bread crumbs
½ cup white wine
1 egg
1 garlic clove, crushed

2 eggs, hard-boiled and peeled
6 to 8 tablespoons sour cream
Nutmeg
1 teaspoon salt
Pepper
1½ cups boiling broth

Mix meats with mushrooms and bread crumbs soaked in white wine and egg. Add salt, pepper, garlic clove, a good pinch of nutmeg and 2 tablespoons sour cream. Mix well. Shape into oblong loaf, molded around the hard-boiled eggs. Spoon 4 tablespoons sour cream over meat loaf. Bake in preheated 400° oven ¾ hour, basting frequently. If necessary, add more sour cream. Remove loaf. Add broth to bottom of pan and scrape drippings from bottom and sides. Mix well. Pour over loaf.

CROWN ROAST OF PORK

12-rib loin of pork, cut into a crown
6 strips bacon

Salt, pepper and flour, mixed
Apple stuffing

Cover tip of each rib bone with aluminum foil to prevent burning while roasting. Wrap strips of bacon around lower part of crown. Rub meat with salt, pepper and flour.

APPLE STUFFING

½ pound ground pork
¼ pound ground veal
¼ cup prepared poultry stuffing mix
1 tablespoon scallion, finely chopped

3 tablespoons parsley, chopped
1 cup apple, peeled and diced
Salt and pepper to taste

Mix all together.

Fill center of crown with apple stuffing. Top with 2 strips of bacon. Cover with aluminum foil for the first hour. Roast in moderate oven — 30 to 35 minutes per pound. Remove aluminum foil from bones before serving. Replace with paper frills.

MILK-BAKED HAM STEAK

2½ pounds sliced uncooked ham
Prepared mustard
1 teaspoon brown sugar
1 tablespoon flour

1½ cups sour cream
Salt
Pepper

Spread ham on both sides with mustard and brown sugar. Put in a buttered baking dish. Over this sprinkle flour. Pour in sour cream, seasoned to taste with salt and white pepper. Cover. Bake in 350° oven 40 minutes, turning ham once after 20 minutes. Remove ham. Stir sauce. Replace ham and serve.

Serve with peas, carrots and dill dough buns (see page 125).

BAKED PORK CHOPS FLORENTINE

6 shoulder pork chops
2 packages frozen spinach, cooked and drained
Flour
3 egg yolks, beaten
Grated cheese
Salt
Pepper

For white sauce:
2 tablespoons butter
3 tablespoons flour
2 cups milk
Salt, pepper

Dredge pork chops with seasoned flour. Sear on both sides over high heat until well browned. Turn frequently. Reduce heat and cover pan. Cook about 30 minutes until chops are tender. Turn frequently. Meanwhile, cook spinach. Keep warm.

Prepare white sauce: Melt butter, stir in flour until thoroughly blended. Slowly add milk, stirring constantly. Add salt and pepper. Stir until thick and smooth.

Arrange hot cooked spinach in shallow, buttered baking dish. Place chops on it. Stir egg yolks into white sauce. Pour over the chops. Sprinkle with grated cheese (any kind). Place in hot (400°) oven or under hot broiler. Brown until cheese bubbles.

MARLENE DIETRICH IN *A Foreign Affair*

KIDNEYS IN MUSTARD SAUCE

5 lamb kidneys, cores removed, sliced rather thick
2 veal kidneys
3 tablespoons butter
1 clove garlic, crushed
4 mushrooms, finely sliced
1 tablespoon dry mustard
1 teaspoon meat glaze
3 tablespoons flour
1½ cups stock
3 tablespoons red wine
2 tablespoons sour cream
Fresh parsley, chopped

Brown kidneys quickly in hot butter. Remove. Add 2 teaspoons butter, garlic, mushrooms, mustard and meat glaze to pan. Remove from heat. Add flour and stock. Return to heat and stir until mixture comes to boil. Add wine and sour cream. Cook slowly 10 minutes. Add kidneys and cook 5 minutes more. Serve in casserole topped with fresh parsley.

SMOKED TONGUE AND KUMQUAT MOUSSE

1 cup smoked ground tongue
2 tablespoons raisins, plumped in warmed Madeira
1 teaspoon parsley, chopped
1 teaspoon celery leaves, chopped
2 teaspoons gelatin
4 tablespoons cold chicken stock
2 eggs, separated
¼ cup whipped cream
48 kumquats, cut in halves
Parsley or mint, finely chopped

Put enough cooked smoked tongue through a food chopper to make 1 cup ground meat. Put the tongue again through the fine blade of chopper with raisins. Stir in chopped parsley and celery leaves. Work mixture with wooden spoon until smooth. Soften gelatin in chicken stock and dissolve over low heat. Combine the puréed tongue and gelatin in pan. Heat thoroughly. Remove mixture from heat. Stir in lightly beaten egg yolks and cool. Stir in whipped cream and stiffly beaten egg whites. Chill mixture in a mold 2 hours, until set. Unmold mousse. Top with kumquats. Sprinkle with finely chopped parsley or mint. Keep chilled until serving time.

LAMB WITH EGGPLANT PURÉE

2 pounds leg of lamb, cubed
3 onions, finely grated
½ cup butter
2 teaspoons tomato paste
1 cup water
Salt and pepper
2 large eggplants, unpeeled
1 cup cream
1 cup milk
¼ cup butter
3 tablespoons Parmesan cheese, grated
½ cup bread crumbs
Parsley, chopped
Green pepper rings, thinly sliced

Brown meat and onions in ½ cup butter over moderate heat. Add tomato paste mixed with water, salt and pepper. Boil a few minutes. Cover. Simmer 2 hours until meat is tender and sauce thick.

Prick eggplants with a fork. Cook in hot (400°) oven until tender. Strip off skins. Mash eggplant. Add cream, milk, ¼ cup butter and Parmesan cheese. Stir in bread crumbs. Taste for seasoning. Mix well. Heat, stirring constantly, until mixture becomes a thick purée. Serve lamb and sauce on eggplant purée. Garnish with parsley and green pepper rings.

BREADED LAMB CHOPS

12 lamb chops
Salt and pepper
1 teaspoon powdered ginger
1 cup bread crumbs
1 cup oil
1½ cups tomato sauce
12 pineapple rings
3 cups Béchamel Sauce
¾ cup grated cheddar cheese
½ teaspoon paprika

Flatten lamb chops lightly. Sprinkle with salt, pepper, ginger and bread crumbs. Heat oil in heavy skillet. Brown chops over low heat 5 minutes each side. Lightly cover bottom of heated ovenproof plate with tomato sauce and remove chops to plate. Top each chop with 1 pineapple ring. Cover pineapple and chops with Béchamel Sauce (see page 137). Sprinkle with cheese and paprika. Brown under broiler.

SHASHLIK

2 pounds boned leg of lean lamb,
    cut in 1½-inch thick pieces
1 large onion, chopped
1 clove garlic, finely chopped
¼ cup vinegar
1½ cups red wine

¼ teaspoon ground cloves
¼ teaspoon cinnamon
6 crushed peppercorns
Fat from lamb
Olive oil

Mix meat with onion and garlic. Combine vinegar, 1 cup red wine, ground cloves, cinnamon and peppercorns. Bring mixture to a boil. Cool. Add remaining cup red wine. Marinate meat and vegetables for at least 4 hours at room temperature.

Remove meat. Dry each piece carefully and brush with olive oil. Thread pieces of meat on long skewers. Separate with thin slices of lamb fat. Place skewers on a rack over a drip pan. Broil very close to broiler flame. Turn to brown on all sides. Baste frequently with pan drippings. Salt the shashlik lightly just before serving. Arrange on heated platter. Slip meat off skewer onto plate. Serve with fluffy boiled rice.

MILK-FED LEG OF LAMB

5 to 6 pounds leg of lamb
    boned and tied
Milk to cover
1 bay leaf
2 whole onions, peeled
10 carrots, scraped
1 cup celery, diced
1 leek, chopped

4 cloves
½ cup butter
1 cup flour
Bouillon
1 cup heavy cream
Salt and pepper
½ cup capers

Barely cover lamb with milk. Add bay leaf, onions, carrots, celery, leek, cloves. Salt and pepper to taste. Cover. Simmer until lamb is done (approximately 2½ hours). Remove lamb. Strain stock.

Heat butter in separate pan. Blend in flour. Simmer a minute or two. Add 2 quarts strained lamb stock to flour mixture. Add hot bouillon if not enough stock. Stir well until bubbling. Dissolve any lumps that may appear. Add cream. Boil slowly 20 minutes. Season

TYRONE POWER AND MYRNA LOY IN *The Rains of Ranchi Pur*

with salt and pepper. Strain. Add capers. Serve with sauce over sliced lamb. Good for a small gangbang.

GAUCHO LAMB

2 pounds lamb cut in 1½-inch cubes	1 teaspoon salt
2 cups red wine	Black pepper, freshly ground
½ cup minced onion	1 cup soft bread crumbs
2 bay leaves	Oil
1 tablespoon Worcestershire	Hot gaucho sauce
1 garlic clove, crushed	Hot cooked saffron rice

Marinate lamb for at least 24 hours in combined wine, onion, bay leaves, Worcestershire, garlic, salt and pepper. Remove meat from marinade. Dip in bread crumbs. Thread on skewers. Sprinkle with oil. Broil under high heat 20 minutes until golden brown. Turn frequently. Serve with gaucho sauce, Arabic rice and pine nuts (see page 73).

GAUCHO SAUCE

2 cups chili sauce	1 tablespoon horseradish
1 tablespoon honey	1 small onion, grated
1 cup catsup	1 tablespoon chopped chutney
1 tablespoon piccalilli	

Mix ingredients in saucepan. Cook over low heat, stirring constantly, for 10 minutes.

PHEASANT IN CREAM

1 pheasant, cleaned	1 tablespoon onion, minced
Milk	3 tablespoons butter
Salt and pepper	1 pint sweet or sour cream
Flour	1 tablespoon lemon juice

Cut pheasant in half down the center of breast. Wash in cold water. Dry with cloth. Cover with milk. Allow to stand at least 30 minutes. Remove from milk and dry. Rub with salt and pepper. Roll in flour. Fry, with onion, in butter until golden brown on all sides. Combine cream and lemon juice. Pour over bird. Cover. Simmer about 45 minutes.

PHEASANT WITH WEINKRAUT

3 young pheasants	1½ quarts cooked sauerkraut
2½ teaspoons salt	2 cups white wine
Pepper	3 apples, peeled, cored and chopped
¾ cup butter	2 tablespoons flour
6 slices bacon, cut in half	

Wash and dry pheasants. Rub inside and out with mixture of salt and pepper. Sauté birds in butter about 15 minutes, until they brown on all sides. Top breasts of pheasants with bacon. Secure with toothpicks. Arrange in casserole. Add butter remaining in pan. Drain sauerkraut. Add wine and apples. Surround birds with sauerkraut mixture. Cover casserole. Cook over low heat until pheasants are tender. Remove to warm plate. Stir flour into sauerkraut. Heat slowly, stirring constantly. Serve pheasants circled by sauerkraut.

ROAST SADDLE OF YOUNG BOAR

1 saddle of young boar	Salt and pepper
1 carrot	Red wine
1 onion, cut in rings	3 tablespoons butter
2 shallots, cut in half	18 chestnuts
Large bunch rosemary	

Marinate boar in carrot, onion, shallots, salt, pepper, rosemary and wine to cover for 3 to 4 hours. Turn meat twice. An hour before roasting, remove from marinade. Dry well. Strain marinade and reserve. Roast in buttered earthenware baking dish in hot (450°) oven 20 minutes. Reduce heat to 350°. Top with 3 tablespoons melted butter. Add ¼ cup heated marinade to roasting dish. Baste frequently, adding hot marinade as needed. Roast 18 minutes per pound. Meanwhile: Boil and skin chestnuts. Add to roast. Cook 15 minutes. Serve chestnuts as a garnish.

ANN SHERIDAN

LANA TURNER

POTATOES STUFFED WITH MUSHROOMS

½ pound mushrooms, peeled
1½ tablespoons chives, chopped
1½ tablespoons bread crumbs
1 large egg, slightly beaten

Salt
Pepper
6 large baking potatoes, peeled
2 tablespoons butter

Cook mushrooms in boiling salted water 15 minutes. Drain. Chop mushrooms. Reserve the water. Combine mushrooms with chives, bread crumbs and egg. Season with salt and pepper. Blend mixture thoroughly. Scoop a little of the pulp out of each potato with an apple corer. Reserve a small outside piece to use as a plug later. Fill each opening with prepared stuffing. Replace small outside piece to "plug" each potato. Place potatoes in a buttered baking dish. Pour in mushroom water. Bake in hot (425°) oven 45 minutes until potatoes are soft. Baste frequently.

SPINACH SOUFFLÉ

Butter for greasing soufflé dish
Parmesan cheese, grated
1 10-ounce package frozen spinach, chopped
4 tablespoons butter
4 tablespoons flour
1 cup milk, boiling

Pinch of salt
⅛ teaspoon nutmeg
¼ teaspoon black pepper
6 egg yolks
6 egg whites
1 teaspoon salt

Butter sides and bottom of soufflé dish. Refrigerate. When chilled, spread again with butter. Sprinkle with Parmesan cheese. Shake off excess. Cook spinach. Cool immediately. Replace spinach in saucepan and heat until all moisture disappears. Spinach *must be dry*. Set aside. Melt butter in a saucepan. Stir in flour. Stir constantly until flour is cooked. Remove from heat and let cool slightly. Stir in half the boiling milk. Mix well. Add remaining milk. Keep stirring with wire whisk until thick and smooth. Mix white sauce, salt, nutmeg, pepper, spinach and egg yolks in blender on high speed until mixed. Beat egg whites with 1 teaspoon salt until stiff. Fold carefully into spinach mixture a little at a time. Fold until mixed. Pour into prepared soufflé dish. Set in pan of boiling water. Bake in preheated oven at 300° 60 minutes, until firm. Serve immediately.

FRESH FRUIT GELATIN

1½ tablespoons gelatin	1 cup water
2 tablespoons cold water	3 tablespoons lemon juice, strained
1 cup white wine	2 pears, peeled and cut in large dice
¼ cup dry sherry	1 cup pitted Bing cherries

Allow gelatin to soften in cold water for 5 minutes. Place over hot water. Stir until thoroughly dissolved. Stir in white wine, sherry, water and lemon juice.

Pour one-inch layer of gelatin mixture into glass serving dish. Set in freezer 10 minutes, until firm. Remove. Arrange pears and cherries on firm gelatin. Add remaining gelatin mixture and chill.

BAKED PINEAPPLE

1 large fresh ripe pineapple	3 tablespoons rum
¼ cup sugar	4 tablespoons butter

Lay pineapple on its side and take off a thick slice that does not include the green top. Carefully scoop out insides and cut into bite-sized pieces. Sweeten to taste with sugar. Flavor with rum. Put pineapple pieces back into pineapple shell. Dot filling with butter. Cover with foil (including green leaves). Bake in a moderate (350°) oven 20 minutes. Bring to table on a plate to serve warm, topped with sauce.

SAUCE

1 pint light cream	1 teaspoon cornstarch
¼ cup sugar	¼ teaspoon salt
1 egg	3 teaspoons white rum
2 egg yolks	

Heat cream to simmer in top of double boiler. Beat sugar with the 1 egg, 2 egg yolks, cornstarch, salt and rum. Add to slowly simmering

MARILYN MONROE

cream. Cook over hot water, stirring constantly, until smooth and slightly thickened. Chill. Serve on top of the pineapple.

CHOCOLATE SOUFFLÉ WITH CRÈME DE CACAO

2 envelopes unflavored gelatin
½ cup water
⅔ cup Crème de Cacao
1¼ cups brown sugar
1 10-ounce package semi-sweet chocolate

1 tablespoon bitter cocoa
6 eggs, separated
½ teaspoon salt
1½ cups heavy cream, whipped

Put a 2-inch waxed paper collar around a 2-quart soufflé dish. Set aside. Mix gelatin, water, crème de cacao and ½ cup sugar over low heat. Stir constantly until gelatin and sugar dissolve. Add chocolate and cocoa. Stir until melted. Remove from heat. Beat in egg yolks, one at a time. Cool. Add salt to egg whites. Beat until stiff. Gradually beat in remaining sugar. Continue beating until very stiff. Fold egg whites into gelatin mixture. Fold in whipped cream. Turn into prepared soufflé dish. Chill for several hours.

RUDOLPH VALENTINO
ITALIAN FOOD

Fagioli con Caviale
(BEANS AND RUSSIAN CAVIAR)

Gnocchi Verdi
(GREEN DUMPLINGS)

Vitello Tonnato
(COLD VEAL WITH TUNA FISH SAUCE)

Scampi alla Marinara
(JUMBO SHRIMP FISHERMAN STYLE)

Scampi al Moro
(JUMBO SHRIMP)

Risotto di Frutti di Mare
(SEAFOOD RISOTTO)

Tonnarelli alla Zingara
(SPAGHETTI TONNARELLI GYPSY STYLE)

Pomodori Ripieni
(STUFFED TOMATOES)

Tacchino Ripieno
(STUFFING FOR TURKEY)

Cozze Marinara
(MUSSELS WITH WHITE WINE)

Risotto Casalingo
(RISOTTO HOME STYLE)

Eggplant Parmigiana

Zabaglione

Spaghetti al Pesto

RUDOLPH VALENTINO IN *Monsieur Beaucaire*

FAGIOLI CON CAVIALE
(Beans and Russian Caviar)

½ pound white beans soaked over-
    night in water to cover
6 tablespoons black caviar
Oil

Salt
Pepper, fresh grated
Lemon quarters

Drain water from beans. Put in pot with 6 cups cold water, no salt. Simmer, covered, very slowly until tender, about 2½ hours. Keep heat as low as possible. This helps prevent beans from breaking.

When ready to serve, remove beans from pot, without liquid. Mix with caviar. Dress with oil, salt and pepper to taste. Serve with lemon quarters.

GNOCCHI VERDI
(Green Dumplings)

---

3 cups cooked, well-drained spinach
3 cups ricotta or dry cottage cheese
4 tablespoons flour
6 tablespoons Parmesan cheese,
    grated
Pinch of nutmeg

Salt
Pepper, freshly ground
2 eggs plus one yolk
½ cup melted butter
Grated cheese

Finely chop thoroughly drained (squeezed dry) spinach. Frozen spinach, finely chopped, is very convenient. Put through food grinder. Mash spinach and ricotta or dry cottage cheese together with flour, Parmesan, nutmeg, salt and pepper until well blended — it should not be lumpy. Stir in beaten eggs. Mix thoroughly. Set in refrigerator about one hour to make handling easier.

Spread pastry board lightly with flour. Dust your hands with flour. Roll mixture into flour, shaping into one-inch by three-inch oblongs, or walnut-sized balls. If they are too light to hold together, add a little more flour. Set aside in the refrigerator until ready to serve.

Then drop gently into a large pot of boiling salted water. They are ready when they float to top of water. Remove carefully with perforated spoon. Place in shallow buttered baking dish. Keep warm until all are cooked. Top with melted butter and lots of grated cheese. Sprinkle generously with freshly grated pepper.

VITELLO TONNATO
(Cold Veal with Tuna Fish Sauce)

2 pounds veal rump	Salt
2 anchovy fillets	Lemon slices
1 cup white wine	*For tuna fish sauce:*
1 or 2 sprigs parsley	Mayonnaise (see page 323)
1 onion	4 ounces tuna fish
1 bay leaf	1 tablespoon anchovy paste
1 celery stalk	2 tablespoons lemon juice
1 carrot	½ cup capers

Make 3 or 4 incisions in meat. Insert pieces of anchovy. Tie meat to keep shape. Place in cold water to cover with wine, parsley, onion, bay leaf, celery, carrot and salt. Bring to a boil. Simmer slowly 1½ to 2 hours until tender. Allow to cool in water.

Prepare tuna fish sauce: Make thick mayonnaise (using 2 eggs). Place with tuna fish, anchovy paste, lemon juice and capers in electric blender. Add enough stock from veal to thin to consistency of thick cream.

Remove veal from stock. Slice thin. Arrange on serving dish. Cover with sauce. Refrigerate at least 3 hours. Serve with sliced lemon.

SCAMPI ALLA MARINARA
(Jumbo Shrimp Fisherman Style)

Tomato sauce (see page 324)
1½ pounds shelled jumbo shrimp
2 minced garlic cloves mashed with 1 tablespoon
    very finely chopped parsley
Salt
Pepper

Prepare tomato sauce. Boil jumbo shrimp in salted water about 10 minutes. Add to tomato sauce, with the mashed garlic and parsley. Simmer slow about 15 minutes.

SCAMPI AL MORO
(Jumbo Shrimp)

Scampi are very similar to our jumbo shrimp, the French *langoustines* and the English Dublin Bay prawns. There is another variety called *mazzencolle,* which is equally good, and a considerably smaller shrimp, often used in *risotto,* called *gamberi.*

Jumbo shrimp, 8 per person	Butter
Olive oil	Lemon juice
Salt and pepper	

Cut shrimp in two, lengthwise, without removing shells. Baste with oil. Rub with salt and pepper. Place in shallow baking dish. Bake in medium hot oven 10 minutes, then dot with butter, a little lemon juice on each, and finish cooking, about 5 minutes. Serve with the juice.

RISOTTO DI FRUTTI DI MARE
(Seafood Risotto)

12 mussels	2 tablespoons olive oil
18 clams	12 shrimp, shelled
3 tablespoons parsley, finely chopped	2 cups rice
1 onion, finely chopped	½ teaspoon saffron
1 garlic clove, minced	½ cup dry white wine
1 celery stalk, chopped	1 tablespoon cognac
4 tablespoons butter	

Steam mussels and clams in 2 cups water with 1 tablespoon parsley. Remove from shells. Strain juices and set aside for later use.

Brown onion, garlic and celery in 2 tablespoons butter, 2 tablespoons olive oil. Add mussels, clams and shrimp. Cook about 2 minutes. Stir in rice for 3 minutes. Dissolve saffron in white wine and cognac. Add to seafood. Add 1 cup heated fish stock. Keep stirring until liquid is absorbed. Pour in remaining fish stock (use hot water to make enough liquid) a little at a time, stirring continuously until absorbed. It is difficult to ascertain the exact quantity of fish stock, since it depends on the quality of the rice, but 4 to 4½ cups will probably do.

When rice is tender and fluffy, remove from heat and stir in 2 tablespoons of butter and remaining parsley.

TONNARELLI ALLA ZINGARA
(Spaghetti Tonnarelli Gypsy Style)

1 pound homemade pasta
or 1 pound spaghetti or very fine egg
   noodles
¼ pound ham
6 tablespoons oil

1 cup sliced sautéed mushrooms
1 cup cooked fine peas
6 tablespoons butter
Parmesan cheese

Cook *pasta* in boiling water until *al dente* — tender but still firm. Cut ham into small fine strips. Heat, do not brown, ham in oil. Add mushrooms, peas and butter. Cook 2 minutes. Add 5 or 6 tablespoons hot water. Heat another minute while draining *pasta*. Serve in heated serving plate. Top with sauce. Garnish with Parmesan cheese.

POMODORI RIPIENI
(Stuffed Tomatoes)

6 large tomatoes
1½ cups uncooked rice
Salt and pepper

¼ teaspoon basil
4 tablespoons olive oil

Cut tops off tomatoes. Scoop out pulp and strain. Mix pulp with rice, salt, pepper, basil and oil. Divide into 6 parts and stuff tomatoes with this mixture. Sprinkle with olive oil. Place in well-oiled baking dish and bake in moderate (350°) oven 1 hour.

TACCHINO RIPIENO
(Stuffing for 12- to 14-Pound Turkey)

1 pound ground pork
1 pound ground hamburg
½ pound fresh Italian sausage
Salt
Pepper
½ loaf Italian bread
Broth or warm water
2 slices Italian ham, diced

4 slices salami, diced
1 medium mozzarella cheese,
   chopped
½ cup celery, diced
½ small onion, chopped
¼ clove garlic, chopped
3 eggs, slightly beaten
Parsley

Sauté first three ingredients until brown. Add salt and pepper. Let stand. Soak bread in ¼ cup broth or warm water until soft, then squeeze thoroughly. Add bread and rest of ingredients to meat mixture. Mix thoroughly with your *hands* until it resembles dog food. Stuff turkey and bake.

COZZE MARINARA
(Mussels with White Wine)

3 quarts mussels	1 clove garlic, crushed
1 small onion, minced	Salt and pepper
¾ cup dry white wine	2 egg yolks
1 bay leaf	¼ cup cream
⅛ teaspoon thyme	3 tablespoons parsley, chopped

Scrub mussels thoroughly. Put in a pan with onion, wine, bay leaf, thyme, garlic and salt. Bring slowly to a boil. Simmer until all the shells are open but not longer than 5 minutes. Discard any unopened mussels. Set aside mussels. Keep warm. Strain off liquor. Reduce by one-third. Remove from heat. Cool slightly. Add egg yolks mixed in cream. Stir over low heat until thickened. Do not boil. Add parsley. Serve mussels with sauce poured over all.

RISOTTO CASALINGO
(Risotto Home Style)

6 chicken livers	¾ cup rice
5 tablespoons butter	2 tablespoons tomato paste
2 onions, chopped	2 cups consommé
4 tablespoons mushrooms, sliced	8 tablespoons grated cheese

Brown livers in hot butter. Remove from pan. Cook onions briskly until they begin to brown. Add mushrooms. Cook a little longer. Add rice, tomato paste and consommé. Cook until rice begins to absorb consommé. Add a little more consommé. Continue cooking until rice has absorbed all the liquid. Stir frequently. Slice livers and mix into rice. Top with grated cheese. Dot with butter. Pile in deep heatproof dish. Put in warm oven a moment. Serve with big bowl of grated cheese.

EGGPLANT PARMIGIANA

1½ pounds eggplant
1 or 2 eggs, beaten
1 teaspoon salt
¼ teaspoon pepper
½ teaspoon oregano
½ cup oil

½ pound mozzarella cheese, sliced thin
2 cups tomato sauce
½ teaspoon dried basil
½ cup grated Parmesan

Wash but do not peel eggplant. Slice thin. Season eggs with salt, pepper and oregano. Beat lightly. Dip eggplant slices in egg. Fry in hot oil ½ inch deep, until golden brown on both sides. Drain on absorbent paper. Arrange layers of eggplant, mozzarella, tomato sauce and basil in baking dish. Sprinkle with grated cheese. Bake in moderate (350°) oven until well heated through — about half an hour.

ZABAGLIONE

6 egg yolks
½ cup sugar

⅔ cup Marsala wine
Ladyfingers

In top pan of double boiler beat egg yolks with sugar until thick and pale. Gradually beat wine into mixture. Place pan over boiling water. Continue beating until mixture foams up and begins to thicken. Serve hot in sherbet glasses with ladyfingers.

SPAGHETTI AL PESTO

1½ cups good fresh basil
½ cup parsley
3 tablespoons pine nuts
1 clove garlic, crushed
3 tablespoons olive oil
Salt and pepper

½ pound spaghettini
4 tablespoons pecorina cheese (strong goat Parmesan), grated
4 tablespoons Parmesan cheese, grated
3 tablespoons butter

In an electric blender, slowly blend basil, parsley, pine nuts and garlic. Add oil, salt and pepper. Blend thoroughly. Meanwhile, boil spaghettini until al dente. Drain, setting aside 2 tablespoons boiling water. Put spaghettini in a heated serving bowl. Mix in water, sauce and cheeses. Add butter and toss thoroughly.

POTPOURRI

- CHICKEN POT PIE
- PIGEON POT COUNTRY STYLE
- HAM HOT POT
- CHICKEN IN THE POT
- MUTTON HOT POT
- OLD-FASHIONED POT ROAST
- POT AU CHOCOLAT
- BEEF POT ROAST
- SPICED POT ROAST
- BLACK BEAN POTAGE
- CHICKEN HASH
- SOUTHERN STYLE HASH
- HASH TARTARE
- CORNED BEEF HASH

- POTTED SHRIMP AND RICE
- POTTED PEA SOUP
- BLACK BEAN POT
- POTS DE CRÈME
- BAKED BEEF HASH
- TURKEY HASH
- HOW TO ROLL A JOINT
- HASH TART
- YORKSHIRE HOT POT
- BROILED LOBSTER HASH
- CREAMED CHICKEN HASH
- CORNED BEEF HASH BURGERS
- ORIGINAL PEPPER POT

HOMAGE TO ALICE B. TOKLAS
- CHOCOLATE FUDGE HASH CANDY
- QUICK CHOCOLATE FUDGE HASH

As a spiritual child of the Forties, I cannot give my imprimatur to this sort of behavior. The drugtaker is a passivist. I am an activist. Yet — to be fair — how can the average person make a meaningful life for himself in an overpopulated world?

— *Myra Breckinridge*, CHAPTER 10

I SMOKED my first marihuana cigarette at the age of sixteen in the second balcony of the Loew's State movie theater on a Saturday morning. It was the first movie in which I saw marvelous Steve Reeves, who later went on to become a foreign film star in *Hercules,* the film that also saw the emergence of Joseph E. Levine as a major film producer-distributor.

Some stud shoved it in my mouth as I sat there gaping at the enormous biceps of sexy Steve. Unaware of what I was doing, I puffed on it, much to the stud's delight, as later he bragged that he had "turned me on." My recollection of that experience was that it was rather pleasant and I surprisingly didn't find myself "hooked" in any way though I must admit that the knowledge of what I had done was somewhat traumatic, particularly when I found out it was illegal. Nevertheless, I avidly tried to avoid the company of those who trafficked in marihuana but time and again, while doing my research, I found myself in the presence of that infamous weed. It was everywhere. And the most unlikely people were indulging in this passive act. One could hardly go anywhere without somebody suddenly whipping out a "joint" (the current euphemism for a cigarette containing marihuana or hashish).

Well aware of what this indulgence could do to the moral fiber of the youth of this country, and wondering how to combat the smoking of this insidious import, I decided to cook with it. The fruits of my experiments and labors are contained herewith. And if it's not exactly your cup of tea, just leave out the pot, even if the children might disapprove.

Recommending the "high" cuisine to any but the best of cooks is difficult since potency and quality are still, to the amateur, unknown factors. Though all of these recipes have been laboratory tested, I cannot honestly say they have the Good Housekeeping Seal of Approval. Still, I am sure they will prove successful for whatever purpose you have in mind, but good as they are, I still wouldn't write home to the kids about them.

CHICKEN POT PIE

2 plump boiling chickens
4 cups dry red wine
2 cups vinegar
2 bay leaves
¼ teaspoon thyme
4 carrots, sliced
1 onion, diced
1 celery stalk, diced
1 teaspoon salt

1 tablespoon peppercorns
1 cup butter
½ cup flour
18 pearl onions
1 pound mushrooms, sliced
3 ounces brandy
2½ teaspoons finely crushed *pot*
(optional)

Marinate chickens overnight in combined wine, vinegar, bay leaves, thyme, sliced carrot, diced onion, celery, salt and peppercorns. Remove from marinade. Strain and save the marinade. Brown chickens in butter in a skillet until golden. Put butter and chickens in deep saucepan. Add flour. Cook 1 minute or until butter and flour mixture is thickened, stirring constantly. Add marinade. Bring to boil. Reduce heat. Cover and simmer 1 hour. Add pearl onions, mushrooms, carrots and *pot*. Simmer for 20 minutes. Stir in brandy. Serve immediately. (Rabbit may be substituted for chicken.)

PIGEON POT COUNTRY STYLE

3 jumbo squabs, cut in half
¾ pound lean beef rump, cut in 6 slices
Flour
⅓ cup butter
3 hard-boiled eggs, peeled and cut in half
1½ teaspoon onion, finely chopped
1½ teaspoon leek (white part only) finely chopped
1½ to 1¾ cups good chicken stock

1 *bouquet garni:*
  1 large bay leaf
  2 sprigs green celery leaves (tops)
  1 sprig thyme
  7 or 8 sprigs parsley
2 cloves
1 teaspoon *pot*, crushed (optional)
1 clove garlic, crushed
1 teaspoon Worcestershire
8 peppercorns
1 teaspoon salt
2 teaspoons *hashish*, grated (optional)
½ box pie crust mix, prepared as directed

Dredge beef and squab halves in flour. Brown in butter on all sides. Arrange pigeons in deep pie dish. Place a slice of beef over each half. Top each with ½ hard-boiled egg. In a separate saucepan slowly cook the onion and leek in the chicken stock. Add the *bouquet garni* tied together with white kitchen thread, cloves, *pot,* garlic, Worcestershire, peppercorns and salt. Pour over pigeons. Add *hashish.* Cover with a rich, flaky pie crust. Make a few slashes on top to allow steam to escape. Brush with cold milk. Bake in moderate (350°) oven 35 to 40 minutes. Serve.

HAM HOT POT

4 tablespoons butter
2½ tablespoons flour
2 cups meat stock or bouillon
2½ teaspoons curry powder
1¾ cups cold, cooked lean ham cubes
1 can small mushroom buttons

6 large green olives, pitted
1 cup freshly shelled peas
Salt and pepper
Large bay leaf
1 tablespoon parsley, chopped
2½ teaspoons *pot,* finely grated (optional)

Blend flour in 3 tablespoons melted butter in flameproof ovenproof casserole. Gradually stir in meat stock until smooth and well blended. Stir in curry powder, mixed with a little cold water. Mix thoroughly. Boil up once. Remove from heat. Add ham, mushrooms, olives, and peas. Season with salt and pepper. Add bay leaf. Cover. Cook in moderate (375°) oven 40 minutes. Add *pot.* Cook 10 minutes more. Remove. Taste for seasoning. Just before serving stir in 1 tablespoon butter and parsley. Serve with boiled rice.

CHICKEN IN THE POT

5 pound hen
6 pieces celery
1 leek
Black pepper, freshly grated
4 quarts water
1 medium-sized onion
6 carrots, scraped

2 medium-sized bay leaves
4 sprigs parsley
Salt
1½ teaspoons *pot* (optional)
½ teaspoon *hashish,* finely grated (optional)

Place everything in large heavy pot with tight-fitting cover. Cook very slowly 2½ to 3 hours, until chicken is very tender but does not fall apart. Remove fat from stock. Serve broth separately. Add 1 table-

spoon sherry to each portion of broth. Reheat chicken and serve with
boiled vegetables, potatoes and horseradish. Season with finely grated
hash.

MUTTON HOT POT

2-pound neck of mutton, boned,
   cut in 6 slices
8 potatoes, thickly sliced
Salt
Pepper
Nutmeg
Thyme
Mace

3 lamb kidneys, cut in 12 thin slices
6 plump fresh oysters
1 cup hot mutton stock
¾ cup boiling water
Butter
2½ teaspoons finely crushed *pot*
   (optional)

Trim skin and most of fat off mutton. Arrange a deep layer of thickly
sliced potatoes in bottom of well-buttered earthenware casserole. Add
mutton slices, slightly overlapping each other. Season to taste with
mixed salt, pepper, nutmeg, thyme and mace. Top each slice with 2
thin slices of lamb kidney and 1 plump oyster. Arrange another layer
of potatoes; then pour in the hot mutton stock (made with trimmings
and mutton bones) and boiling water. Season with salt and pepper.
Top with melted butter. Cover with buttered paper and bake in moderate (350°) oven 1¼ hours. Mix in *pot*. Remove paper and continue
baking 20 to 25 minutes longer, or until top is delicately browned and
crisp. Serve directly from baking dish.

OLD-FASHIONED POT ROAST

4 pounds bottom round of beef
4 cups dry red wine
1 teaspoon grated *hashish* (optional)
Salt and pepper
¼ cup oil
1 medium-sized onion, sliced
3 medium-sized carrots, diced
2 large celery stalks, diced
1 leek, diced
¼ cup mushrooms, sliced
¼ cup flour

¼ teaspoon dried basil
1 bay leaf
3 fresh tomatoes, diced
1 Number 2 can tomato purée
2 garlic cloves, crushed
1 tablespoon sweet paprika
1 tablespoon celery salt
1½ teaspoons *pot*, crushed (optional)
1½ quarts stock

Marinate meat in wine with *hash* about 6 hours. Turn several times. Remove and set marinade aside. Tie meat securely with string. Wipe dry. Season with salt and pepper. Heat oil in heavy braising pot until smoking. Brown meat on all sides. Add onion, carrots, celery, leek and mushrooms. Sauté vegetables until brown. Add flour and brown again. Mix well. Add marinade, basil, bay leaf, tomatoes, purée, garlic, paprika, celery salt, ½ the *pot* and stock. Bring to boil. Skim off foam and excess fat. Cover tightly. Bake in 375° oven 2½ hours until meat is well done. Add remaining *pot* for the last half-hour. Remove from oven. Strain sauce. Serve meat sliced. Good with hashed potatoes.

POT AU CHOCOLAT

½ pound dark sweet chocolate, broken in small pieces
5 tablespoons cold water
4 egg yolks
2 teaspoons rum

1 teaspoon grated *hashish* (optional)
½ teaspoon *pot*, finely crushed (optional)
5 egg whites

Put chocolate in heavy pan with cold water. Stir over low heat until dissolved. Remove from heat. Mix in, carefully, the egg yolks, rum, *hashish* and *pot*. Fold in stiffly beaten egg whites. Mix well. Pour into small glasses. Refrigerate for at least 4 hours.

BEEF POT ROAST

4 pounds pot roast
Salt and pepper
2 tablespoons flour
4 tablespoons butter
¼ cup red wine

3 onions, sliced
2 tablespoons tomato paste
2 cups water
1 bay leaf
2½ teaspoons *pot* (optional)

Season meat with salt and pepper. Rub with flour. Brown meat well on all sides in melted butter in a Dutch oven. Add wine and sliced onions. Sauté until onions soften. Add tomato paste, dissolved in the water, and bay leaf. Cover and simmer for 3 hours. Add *pot* ½ hour before done. Serve with mashed potatoes or cooked rice.

SPICED POT ROAST

½ teaspoon red pepper, crushed
8 garlic cloves
½ teaspoon cumin, ground
1 teaspoon powdered mustard
¾ teaspoon turmeric, ground
1¼ teaspoons ground ginger
1 tablespoon lemon pulp
1¼ tablespoons sugar
1 teaspoon salt
3 tablespoons poppy seeds
½ cup vinegar

2 pounds beef or lamb, cut in large cubes
1 small onion, finely sliced
4 tablespoons shortening
2 cloves
2 bay leaves
1 cup tomato purée
1½ teaspoons *pot*, finely crushed (optional)
1 teaspoon *hashish*, finely grated (optional)

Place crushed red pepper, garlic, cumin, mustard, turmeric, ginger, lemon pulp, sugar, salt, poppy seeds and vinegar in electric blender. Blend at high speed 2 to 3 minutes. Marinate meat 2 hours in blended spices. Fry onion until soft in shortening with cloves and bay leaves. Turn off heat. Allow oil to become lukewarm. Add meat. Simmer meat until half cooked — almost 1 hour. Strain off oil. Add to tomato purée and *pot* and *hash*. Cook on high heat until meat is tender, about ½ hour. Serve.

NOTE: Duck, small chickens or shrimp may be substituted.

BLACK BEAN POTAGE

8 slices bacon, finely chopped
1 cup onion, finely chopped
½ cup leeks, finely chopped
½ cup carrots, chopped
1 cup butter
1 pound canned black beans

1 ham bone
3 quarts chicken broth
2 cups chopped mustard greens
8 frankfurters, skinned and sliced
1½ teaspoons *hashish* (optional)
Salt and pepper

Fry bacon with onions, leeks and carrots. Cook until limp, about 10 minutes. If it becomes dry, add butter to avoid burning. Add black beans with ham bone and broth. Cook 1 hour. Add mustard greens. Cook 1½ hours. Remove ham bone. Divide soup in half. Blend half in blender with *hashish*. Mix into remaining half. Cut meat from bone in very fine pieces. Add to soup. Add frankfurters. Boil 5 minutes. Season lightly with salt and pepper to taste. Serve in heated soup tureen with buttered croutons.

CHICKEN HASH

3 ounces butter
10 mushrooms, diced
½ cup sherry
2 cups Béchamel
1 cup cream
4 pounds cooked chicken, diced
2 teaspoons *hashish*, finely grated (optional)
3 egg yolks

Salt and pepper
2 cups cooked rice
⅓ cup Parmesan cheese
For Béchamel:
  2 tablespoons butter
  2 heaping tablespoons flour
  2 cups milk, heated
  1 pinch salt
  1 pinch nutmeg

Prepare Béchamel: Heat butter. Add flour and ½ teaspoon *hashish*. Mix well until smooth and all lumps have disappeared. Add milk, salt and nutmeg. Cook 15 to 20 minutes.

Sauté mushrooms in butter until lightly brown. Add sherry. Cover. Reduce liquid by one-third. Mix in Béchamel, cream chicken and remaining *hashish*. Simmer slowly 5 minutes. Thicken with egg yolk. Salt and pepper to taste. Spread rice in casserole. Cover rice with chicken mixture. Sprinkle with Parmesan. Brown under broiler.

SOUTHERN STYLE HASH

2 small green peppers, diced
4 medium-size onions, diced
3 large stalks celery, diced
1 Number 2 can tomatoes
2 pounds lean fresh ground pork
3 tablespoons butter
1 package noodles, cooked

Salt
Pepper
1 to 2½ teaspoons *pot*, crushed (optional)
1 cup grated cheese
1 cup cracker meal

Put green peppers, onions and celery in a stew pot. Add tomatoes. Cook slowly 10 to 15 minutes, stirring frequently. Cook pork in butter until lightly brown. Mix noodles with grated cheese. Add to vegetables. Add ground pork. Season highly with salt and pepper. Turn into greased baking dish. Bake in moderate (350°) oven about 20 minutes. Remove and sprinkle with *pot*, top with grated cheese mixed with cracker meal. Continue baking 15 minutes more, until brown.

If you're not going to use the *pot*, then be real Southern and add sautéed mushrooms.

HASH TARTARE

2 pounds ground beef
2 eggs
½ cup capers
½ cup onion, minced
1 garlic clove, crushed
1 teaspoon Worcestershire

2 teaspoons *hashish*, finely grated (optional)
2 teaspoons salt
Black pepper, freshly ground
Pumpernickel bread

Mix ingredients together. Serve raw with thinly sliced pumpernickel.

CORNED BEEF HASH

3 cups canned corned beef hash
3 tablespoons catsup
1 teaspoon dried onion flakes
1 tablespoon bacon fat

2 teaspoons *hashish* (optional) or substitute:
½ teaspoon oregano

Combine beef hash, catsup, dried onion flakes and *hashish* thoroughly. Sauté in bacon fat in covered skillet over low heat 10 minutes.

POTTED SHRIMP AND RICE

6 tablespoons vegetable shortening
3 cups shrimps, cleaned and deveined
2 medium onions, thinly sliced
2 large tomatoes, sliced thick
6 green bell peppers, sliced in rings
1½ teaspoons *pot*, finely crushed (optional)

Salt to taste
5 cups hot cooked rice
1 cup cooked peas
½ cup cooked carrots, diced
1 two-egg omelet, chopped
Butter or margarine
1 medium onion, thinly sliced

Heat shortening in skillet. Fry shrimp, onion, tomato, peppers and *pot* until almost dry. Add salt. In mixing bowl, combine rice, peas, carrots and chopped omelet. Spread the egg and vegetable mixture over the shrimp mixture. Dot with butter or margarine. Cover. Cook slowly a few minutes until butter has melted. Crisp-fry onions. Garnish with onion rings.

POTTED PEA SOUP

¼ cup butter
1 medium-size onion, sliced
2 small pieces celery, sliced
1 pound quick-cooking green split peas
1 whole ham bone
3 pints chicken or beef stock
½ bay leaf

1½ teaspoons black pepper, crushed
⅛ teaspoon sugar
Salt
1 cup heavy cream
2 teaspoons *hashish*, grated (optional)
Croutons

Melt butter in heavy kettle with onion and celery. Simmer 5 minutes. Add peas, ham bone, stock, bay leaf, pepper, sugar and salt. Add meat cut from bone. Cook 1½ hours on slow heat. Remove bone. Strain through fine sieve. Add cream. Add *hashish*. Reheat.

Serve with croutons floating on top.

BLACK BEAN POT

2 to 3 cans cooked black beans
½ pound salt pork, sliced
1 small ham bone
1 quart water
1 onion, minced
½ clove garlic, chopped fine
½ carrot, diced
5 tablespoons fat

1 bay leaf, crushed
Pinch thyme
¼ teaspoon nutmeg
Salt and pepper
1 teaspoon *hashish*, grated (optional)
2 tablespoons brown sugar, warmed
1 teaspoon *pot*, crushed (optional)
½ cup rum

Place beans in heavy iron pot with salt pork, ham bone and water. Boil slowly. Meanwhile, sauté onion, garlic and carrot in fat in a separate skillet. Add to pot. Add bay leaf, thyme, nutmeg and *hash*. Cover and cook slowly 3 hours. Add sugar, *pot*, and rum. Season to taste. Mix well and serve.

POTS DE CRÈME

1 package sweet cooking chocolate
1 teaspoon instant espresso coffee
1½ cups light cream
¼ cup sugar
6 egg yolks, slightly beaten
1 teaspoon vanilla
1 teaspoon *hashish*, grated (optional)
1 teaspoon *pot*, finely crushed (optional)

Combine chocolate, instant espresso, cream and sugar in top of double boiler. Heat over hot water until chocolate melts. Remove from heat. Pour chocolate over the egg yolks — *very slowly*, stirring constantly, until well mixed. Return to double boiler. Continue cooking over hot water stirring constantly until consistency of a thin pudding. Stir in vanilla, *hashish* and *pot*. Turn into individual serving cups. Cool.

BAKED BEEF HASH

4 cups leftover roast beef, diced
¼ cup onion, finely chopped
¼ cup butter
1 cup dry red wine
6 large boiled potatoes, diced
½ cup heavy cream
2 tablespoons soy sauce
2 tablespoons parsley, chopped
¼ teaspoon ground thyme
¼ teaspoon ground savory
1 teaspoon *hashish*, finely grated (optional)
1 teaspoon *pot*, crushed (optional)
Hot paprika

Sauté onion in butter until tender with diced beef and all the ingredients except paprika. Mix well. Turn into casserole. Sprinkle generously with hot paprika. Bake in moderate (350°) oven 30 minutes.

TURKEY HASH

4 tablespoons butter
2 tablespoons flour
½ cup heavy cream
2 teaspoons *hashish*, grated (optional) or substitute:
½ teaspoon oregano
3 cups cooked turkey, diced
½ cup soft bread crumbs
½ cup green pepper, chopped
½ cup onion, chopped
2 tablespoons parsley, chopped
½ teaspoon ground sage
½ teaspoon salt
Black pepper, freshly ground

Melt 2 tablespoons of butter in saucepan, blend in flour, cream and *hashish*. Stir until thickened. Add turkey and all the other ingredients except remaining butter. Melt butter in large skillet. Add turkey mixture. Sauté uncovered 25 minutes. Brown under broiler before serving.

HOW TO ROLL A JOINT
(Boned Leg of Lamb)

1 boned, rolled leg of lamb (about 5 pounds)
Salt and pepper
3 garlic cloves, crushed
1 teaspoon *pot*, finely crushed (optional)
2 4-ounce cans sliced mushrooms with liquid
1½ cups onions, chopped
2 teaspoons *hashish*, finely grated (optional)

Place roast fat side down, unrolled. Sprinkle with salt, pepper, 2 cloves garlic and *pot*. Roll. Secure with kitchen cord and picks. Rub with salt and pepper and remaining garlic. Roast, fat side up, on rack in shallow roasting pan, in 325° oven, 25 minutes per pound for rare, 28 minutes per pound for medium, 30 minutes per pound for well done. 1 hour before done, remove rack. Set roast in pan with mushrooms and their liquid, onions, pan drippings and *hashish*. Baste frequently until done. Serves 10 to 12.

HASH TART

3 cups cooked roast beef, chopped
1 onion, chopped
1 green pepper, seeded and chopped
½ cup seedless raisins
1 teaspoon Worcestershire
Salt and pepper to taste
2 tablespoons whiskey

Roast beef gravy
2 cups mashed potatoes
1 cup Cheddar, grated
¼ cup chives, finely chopped
2 teaspoons *hashish*, finely grated (optional)

Combine roast beef with onion, green pepper, raisins, Worcestershire, salt and pepper. Moisten with whiskey and a little roast beef gravy. Cover with mashed potatoes combined with ½ cup Cheddar, chives and *hashish.* Sprinkle potatoes with ½ cup more grated cheese. Bake hash in very hot (450°) oven until thoroughly heated and potato crust is nicely browned.

YORKSHIRE HOT POT

6 loin lamb chops	1 dozen small potato balls
2 tablespoons butter	½ cup green beans, cut in
2 cups milk	small pieces
2 cups light cream	Salt
1 large bay leaf	Pepper
1 clove garlic, crushed	2½ teaspoons *pot*, finely
1 whole clove	crushed (optional)
1 dozen small white onions, peeled	2 tablespoons flour
1 dozen small mushrooms, caps	Cold milk
peeled and stems thinly sliced	2 egg yolks, slightly beaten

Brown chops on both sides in butter. Meanwhile, scald milk and light cream with bay leaf, garlic and clove. Strain. Then transfer chops to heavy stew pot and add scalded milk and cream. Add onions and mushrooms. Cover. Cook 20 minutes. Add potato balls and green beans. Season with salt, pepper, 1 teaspoon *pot*. Cook 15 to 20 minutes longer. Arrange chops and vegetables on heated platter. Strain milk gravy into another saucepan. Thicken with flour stirred with a little cold milk and remaining *pot*. Bring to boil. Remove pan from heat. Beat in egg yolks. Taste for seasoning. Strain sauce over chops and vegetables.

BROILED LOBSTER HASH

2-pound live lobster	1 teaspoon paprika
2 tablespoons butter	2½ teaspoons *hashish* (optional)
Dash salt	½ cup melted butter
Dash black pepper	1 lemon

Plunge live lobster into vigorously boiling water for 5 minutes. Remove. Allow to cool sufficiently to handle. Split down the middle. Remove entrails. Arrange on heavy broiler pan, meat side up. Make mixture of butter, salt, pepper, paprika and *hashish.* Spread over all of meat. Broil, using 500° heat, 20 minutes. Serve at once with melted butter and lemon quarters.

CREAMED CHICKEN HASH

2 large finely diced green peppers
3 cups concentrated cream of chicken soup
1½ cups cream
5 cups cooked chicken, finely diced

2 teaspoons finely grated *hashish* (optional)
1 teaspoon salt
½ teaspoon pepper, freshly ground

Simmer peppers about 5 minutes in cup of water. Drain. Slowly simmer chicken soup with cream over low heat. Stir in chicken, peppers, *hashish* and seasoning. Stir well, and continue to cook until thoroughly hot. Serve on toast triangles or in shells.

CORNED BEEF HASH BURGERS

3 pounds lean, well-done corned beef brisket
3 tablespoons onions, finely chopped
2 tablespoons butter

3 cups boiled or canned potatoes, finely diced
Dash of pepper
2 teaspoons *hashish*, grated (optional)

Grind corned beef very fine. Brown onions gently in butter. Mix corned beef well with potatoes, slightly browned onions, pepper and *hashish*. Should mixture be too dry, add a little cold water. Shape into 6 patties. Brown in butter on both sides. Serve with a poached egg on top. Garnish with more grated *hash* if desired.

Canned corned beef can be substituted for fresh corned beef.

ORIGINAL PEPPER POT

½ teaspoon crushed red pepper
8 garlic cloves
½ teaspoon ground cumin
1 teaspoon powdered mustard
¾ teaspoon ground turmeric
1¼ teaspoons ground ginger
1 tablespoon lemon pulp
1½ tablespoons sugar
1 teaspoon salt
3 tablespoons poppy seeds

½ cup vinegar
2 pounds beef, cut in large cubes
4 tablespoons vegetable shortening
2 cloves
4 bay leaves
1 small onion, finely sliced
½ cup tomato purée
1½ teaspoons ground *hashish* (optional)
1 teaspoon *pot* (optional)

Place crushed red pepper, garlic, cumin, mustard, turmeric, ginger, lemon pulp, sugar, salt, poppy seeds and vinegar in high speed blender. Blend at high speed 2 to 3 minutes. Place meat in large bowl. Pour blended spices over meat. Marinate 2 hours. Heat vegetable shortening in Dutch oven or casserole. Add cloves and bay leaves. Fry 3 to 4 minutes. Add onion and fry until soft. Turn off heat. Allow oil to become lukewarm. Add meat. Simmer meat until half cooked. Add tomato purée. Increase heat and cook until meat is tender, approximately 40 minutes. Strain off oil. Add *hash* and *pot*. Cook another 20 minutes.

HOMAGE TO
ALICE B. TOKLAS

Between a beautiful girl and an unattractive man I shall always be drawn, like any healthy-minded woman, to the girl.
— *Myra Breckinridge*, CHAPTER 20

ALICE, although I never dated her, was, I am told, one of the most enchanting people that ever lived. She turned out to be an innovator, breaking new ground with the publication of her by now famous cookbook, which includes the worldwide famous recipe for hash fudge. In all deference to lovely Alice, who lived in a more leisurely world than the one we are forced to cope with today, she was not able to take advantage of the many time and labor-saving devices that through the auspices of our local television stations make themselves available to us. Her recipe is a little long and a little arduous. I took it upon myself, but always with the thought of Alice B. in the background, to improve upon it and make it more up-to-date. I realize that there are amongst us those traditionalists who might resent any tampering with a classic, yet I am sure dear Alice, being a levelheaded girl, would thoroughly approve. It is with a clear conscience and total respect for Alice B. that I give to you my two new recipes — Chocolate Fudge Hash Candy and Quick Chocolate Fudge Hash — which I dedicate to the memory of Gertrude Stein.

CHOCOLATE FUDGE HASH CANDY

2 squares unsweetened chocolate
¾ cup milk
1 tablespoon light corn syrup
2 cups sugar
Dash of salt
1 teaspoon *hashish*, finely grated (optional)

1 teaspoon *pot*, finely crushed (optional)
½ cup butter
½ teaspoon vanilla
1 cup walnuts, coarsely chopped

Cook chocolate and milk over low heat, stirring constantly, until smooth and blended. Add corn syrup, sugar, salt, *hashish* and *pot*. Cook, stirring, until sugar dissolves and mixture boils. Lower heat and keep simmering, without stirring, until a small soft ball forms when dropped into cold water. (If you've a candy thermometer, heat until 234°). Remove from heat. Add butter and vanilla. Cool to lukewarm. Then beat mixture until thick and *no longer* glossy. Stir in nuts. Turn into buttered shallow pan. When cold, cut in squares. Makes 18 pieces.

QUICK CHOCOLATE FUDGE HASH

1 box brownie mix
1 teaspoon *hashish*, finely grated (optional)
1 teaspoon *pot*, finely crushed (optional)

Prepare brownie mix as directed on package for making fudge. Mix in *hash* and *pot*. Cook as directed on package.

CHARLES LAUGHTON IN *Sign of the Cross*

QUICK SEDUCTIONS – NOTHING IN THE HOUSE FOOD

- BILLI-BI
- ICED CHICKEN AND CURRY SOUP, SENEGALESE STYLE
- POTAGE CHAMPAGNE
- FRENCH ONION SOUP
- NINO'S WHITE BEAN SOUP
- GRATINÉE LYON
- NEAPOLITAN BROCHETTES
- BEDSPREADS
- BREAD CRUMB OMELET
- TOMATO PIE
- EGGS PARMENTIER
- EGG CURRY
- MACARONI GOULASH
- GARLIC MACARONI
- SPAGHETTI AND GREEN SAUCE

- SPAGHETTI ALLA CARBONARA
- PIEDMONT GNOCCHI
- POTATO BLINTZES
- GNOCCHI SEMOLINA
- SALMON CAVIAR
- TRUITS AMANDINES
- KENNEDY CLAM CHOWDER
- ZUCCHINI SOUFFLÉ
- VEAL CHOPS ENVELOPPÉ
- BEEF PAGLIA
- QUICK CREAMED CHICKEN HASH
- CHICKEN POACHED IN CHAMPAGNE
- CHICKEN LICKEN
- CHICKEN GRÉGOIRE
- CANDLELIGHT PEACHES

SIMPLE seductions are not easy. Rarely planned, they just happen. A ride on the subway, a walk through the park followed by the invariable invitation to a drink or two — one just never knows when opportunity knocks. The postman may not always ring twice, so strike while the iron is hot. Your door's peephole can well be the glory hole of your future. How disastrous to think that all would be lost if one didn't know that the first element of the successful simple seduction is . . . the can opener. That is why a great cook is never caught with his pants down. You must always be prepared, even if it is only a jar of peanut butter or a tube of jelly. This is one of the first dictums of the kitchen. I have always made sure that my cupboard is never bare, even if it only contains the barest elements necessary for the low cuisine. Indeed, I have sometimes been just as lucky with a sardine as when I'd prepared enough food to feed the whole of Coxey's Army. Though the ingredients at hand may be minuscule, ingenuity can produce miracles. Something good enough to eat can always be whipped up. There is virtually no limit to what can be teased out of yesterday's leftovers to produce this evening's feast. Don't give up easily: add a little spice to it, shove it in the oven, simmer it, serve it over ice cubes, cover it with jelly, garnish it with gravy, squeeze a syrup out of it . . . a little knowledge and a lot of imagination can make the highway of life a roller coaster ride. You need only remember that, like *The Bluebird* (one of the rare stinkeroos to have come out of Hollywood during its golden period: 1935–1945), "Happiness is in your own backyard," and if you can't find it there, Buster, then you've got a problem.

ROBERT TAYLOR IN *Stand by for Action*

BILLI-BI

2 quarts mussels
1 cup dry white wine
5 or 6 sprigs of parsley
2 bay leaves
2 cloves garlic, crushed

1 pint milk
6 egg yolks, well beaten
1 cup heavy cream
1 tablespoon butter

Steam mussels in skillet with wine, parsley, bay leaves and garlic. Cover skillet. Place over high heat until mussels open. Strain mussels. Save stock. Trim and discard horny beard from mussels. Strain stock into saucepan. Discard sediment. Add mussels and milk. Bring to a boil. Stir in egg yolks, cream and butter. Heat. Do not let boil.

ICED CHICKEN AND CURRY SOUP, SENEGALESE STYLE

3 tablespoons butter
1 onion, finely chopped
1 apple, peeled and sliced
2 teaspoons curry powder
4 tablespoons flour
½ cup undiluted cream of pea soup

Salt
Chili pepper
Cayenne pepper
3 cups strong chicken stock
1½ cups cream
1 cup white chicken, finely diced

Soften onion and sliced apple in melted butter. Cook very slowly until soft without browning. Add curry powder. Cook slowly 5 to 6 minutes. Slowly stir in flour and pea soup. Add salt, chili pepper and cayenne pepper. Add stock. Stir until smooth. Stir over heat until soup comes to boil. Rub through fine strainer. Refrigerate until very cold. Add cream and chicken. Serve in bowls surrounded by crushed ice. This may be served hot as well as cold.

POTAGE CHAMPAGNE

1 can condensed cream of chicken
    soup
1 cup light cream
2 teaspoons curry powder
¼ cup champagne or dry white wine

2 tablespoons lemon juice
½ teaspoon salt
Black pepper, freshly ground
Chives or parsley, chopped

Blend chicken soup and cream in saucepan. Stir until smooth. Mix curry powder with wine. Add to soup mixture. Simmer over low heat 10 minutes, stirring frequently. Remove from heat. Stir in lemon juice, salt and pepper. Chill in refrigerator for at least 1 hour. Serve garnished with chopped chives or parsley. Add more wine if desired. Serves 2.

FRENCH ONION SOUP

5 large onions, thinly sliced
3 tablespoons olive or salad oil
1 tablespoon butter or margarine
1 tablespoon flour
6 cups chicken bouillon

Salt and pepper to taste
½ teaspoon sugar
4 slices toast, rubbed with garlic
4 tablespoons cheese, grated

Sauté onions in oil very slowly until soft. Add butter. When melted, sprinkle with flour. Stir until golden. Mix bouillon, salt, pepper and sugar. Add to onions. Simmer 10 minutes. Pour into 1 large or 4 individual small casseroles. Float toast on top. Sprinkle with cheese. Heat in moderate (375°) oven 12 minutes. Serve piping hot. Sprinkle with more cheese at table. Serves 4 as a main dish, 6 as a first course.

NINO'S WHITE BEAN SOUP

5 cups canned or cooked white
    beans, with liquid
2 garlic cloves
4 tablespoons olive oil
4 tablespoons parsley
Salt to taste

Black pepper to taste, coarsely
    ground
Bouillon
6 slices toast, rubbed with 3 garlic
    cloves

Heat beans with garlic, olive oil, parsley, salt and pepper. Add enough soup liquid (and/or bouillon) to cover. Blend half in electric blender. Reheat. Place one slice garlic-rubbed toast in each soup plate. Cover with beans, top with blended soup. Season again — and be prepared for a delightful gourmet soup meal. Serves 2.

GRATINÉE LYON

8 thick slices stale bread	Few grains nutmeg
1 tablespoon butter or margarine	¼ cup cheese, grated
3 cups consommé or bouillon	2 eggs
1 bay leaf	2 tablespoons either cognac, rum,
1 teaspoon parsley, chopped	red wine or sherry
Salt and pepper to taste	

Break bread into small pieces. Melt butter in saucepan. Add bread and fry until golden. Pour in hot bouillon. Add bay leaf, parsley, salt, pepper and nutmeg. Cover. Simmer gently 20 minutes. Discard bay leaf. Season to taste. Pour into 2 individual casseroles. Sprinkle each serving with cheese. Brown under broiler about 8 minutes. Slip 1 well-beaten egg into each casserole just before serving. Add cognac, rum or sherry to each. This is a good late-winter-night warmer for two.

OR: Pour into 1 large serving casserole. Add all the cheese. Brown under broiler. Slip 1 beaten egg only into the soup just before serving. (Do not stir soup after the egg has been added).

NEAPOLITAN BROCHETTES

8 thick slices bread, preferably French or Italian
½ pound cheese, Swiss, Edam, Münster or processed American
4 tiny firm tomatoes
½ cup milk seasoned with salt and pepper
1 cup flour
1 egg, lightly beaten
1 cup oil, lard or fat

Cut bread (crusts removed) and cheese into 1 x ½-inch pieces. String on 8 skewers alternating bread, cheese, tomatoes, repeating until skewers are filled. Dip into milk, then flour, then egg. Fry in hot oil until golden brown on all sides. Serves 2.

Variation: Eggplant, zucchini, leftover boiled or canned potatoes, parboiled onions and/or bacon may be added.

BEDSPREADS

4 slices bread	Salt
4 slices lean ham	Pepper
4 eggs, separated	2 tablespoons cooking oil
¼ pound Gruyère, grated	

Trim bread and ham same size. Mix egg yolk with grated Gruyère, salt and pepper, and spread mixture on each slice of bread. Top with piece of ham. Whip egg whites very stiff and make a dome of egg whites (use a soup spoon) on the ham. Heat oil in pan. Add bread, ham and cheese. Heat through. Spoon a little oil onto the whites. Do not brown. Serve at once. Serves 2.

BREAD CRUMB OMELET

1½ cups soft bread crumbs	Dash cayenne
1¾ cups boiling milk	Dash powdered clove
4 eggs, separated	2 tablespoons chives or onion,
½ teaspoon salt	chopped
¼ teaspoon pepper	2 tablespoons butter or margarine

Beat bread crumbs with boiling milk. Add well-beaten egg yolks. Season with salt, pepper, cayenne and clove. Beat until smooth. Stir in chopped chives. Fold in stiffly beaten egg whites. Melt butter in heavy skillet. Add egg mixture. Cook over low heat until bottom and edges of omelet are delicate golden brown and top is puffy — about 7 minutes. Finish cooking in moderate (325°) oven 15 minutes until top is dry. This is wonderful topped with cold cottage cheese, folded over and served on a hot platter.

TOMATO PIE

½ package piecrust mix
6 large tomatoes, cut in ½-inch slices
Salt and pepper to taste
½ cup corn meal

4 tablespoons butter
1 teaspoon sugar
½ cup cheese, grated
1 tablespoon melted butter

Prepare piecrust as directed on package for 1 crust. Season tomatoes with salt and pepper. Coat with cornmeal. Fry in butter. Turn with spatula to brown both sides. Sprinkle each slice with pinch of sugar. Line a pie pan with pastry dough. Place a layer of tomatoes on bottom. Sprinkle with grated cheese. Repeat a layer of tomatoes, then cheese. Continue until tomatoes are used up. Top with cheese. Sprinkle with melted butter. Bake in hot (425°) oven 10 minutes. Lower heat, bake 15 minutes more. Serve piping hot. Serves 2. If you've any Swiss or American cheese slices, add them between each layer.

EGGS PARMENTIER

6 medium boiled potatoes, peeled
4 tablespoons butter or margarine
4 eggs

¾ cup half-and-half cream, plus hot
   milk for potatoes
½ teaspoon salt
¼ teaspoon paprika

Mash boiled peeled potatoes with 3 tablespoons butter and enough hot milk to make smooth and creamy. Arrange in shallow greased baking dish. With bottom of water glass, make 4 deep depressions in potato. Break an egg into each depression. Pour half-and-half cream over all. Season with salt, paprika and dot with remaining butter. Bake in moderate (375°) oven until lightly browned and eggs are set, about 15 minutes.

OR: Place a slice of fried ham in each potato depression, then add egg. Sprinkle with grated cheese before placing in oven. This makes 4 servings.

EGG CURRY

1 tablespoon butter or margarine	Pinch sugar
1 small onion, chopped	¼ teaspoon dry mustard
¼ cup green pepper, chopped	1 Number 2 can tomatoes
1 tablespoon parsley, minced	½ cup boiling water
1 tablespoon curry powder	4 hard-cooked eggs, sliced
1 teaspoon salt	1 cup cooked peas

Sauté onion, green pepper and parsley in butter. Blend in curry powder, salt, sugar, dry mustard. Add tomatoes and boiling water. Stir until well blended and very smooth. Reduce heat. Add eggs and peas. Cover. Simmer very gently — about 15 minutes. Serve on boiled rice. Serves 4.

MACARONI GOULASH

¼ pound elbow macaroni	2 tablespoons sharp cheese
Boiling salted water	Salt
1½ tablespoons butter	Pepper
¾ pound top round beef, ground	
1 can condensed cream of tomato soup	

Dice cheese. While macaroni is boiling in salted water — 9 to 10 minutes — melt butter in a skillet and sauté beef rapidly. Break it up as finely as possible with fork. The beef should be done about the time the macaroni is ready. Drain macaroni, add it to meat. Pour on the soup. Mix thoroughly. Add diced cheese, salt and pepper. Simmer goulash slowly for another 10 minutes, until the cheese is well melted and stirred in. Serves 2.

GARLIC MACARONI

1 pound macaroni or spaghetti	*For sauce:*
4 quarts boiling salted water	15 to 20 cloves garlic, peeled
	4 tablespoons olive oil
	¼ teaspoon basil
	1 tablespoon parsley
	Salt and pepper

Boil macaroni in salted water until *al dente* (firm, but not too soft).

Garlic sauce: This is a recipe for the more adventurous. If you like garlic, you're in for a real treat. If you're the timid type, use only 15 garlic cloves — but not less. Cook the garlic in oil with basil and parsley until golden brown and soft. Mash all together to make a smooth paste. Season to taste. Mix well. Toss with boiled, drained macaroni. Serve in preheated casserole — no cheese!

This is the kind of dish you must share with good friends or spend the evening alone. (And it may be worth it at that.)

This is a good quick main course for 4 — with a crisp, cold salad.

SPAGHETTI AND GREEN SAUCE

1 pound spaghetti	½ cup fresh parsley, chopped
4 quarts boiling salted water	¼ teaspoon black pepper
6 tablespoons olive or salad oil	3 tablespoons butter or margarine
4 cloves garlic, finely chopped	Cheese, grated

While spaghetti is boiling in salted water, sauté garlic in oil until golden. Add parsley and black pepper. Simmer a few minutes. When spaghetti is *al dente* (firm, not too soft), drain thoroughly. Pour into heated bowl with butter. Add sauce. Mix thoroughly. Serve sprinkled with grated cheese. Serves 4.

SPAGHETTI ALLA CARBONARA

1 pound spaghetti	Pinch of oregano
4 quarts boiling salted water	2 eggs
8 to 10 slices bacon	½ cup cheese, grated
1 tablespoon olive oil	Salt and pepper to taste
1 pod tiny red pepper	4 tablespoons melted butter

While spaghetti is boiling in salted water, fry bacon with olive oil, red pepper and oregano until bacon is crisp. Remove pepper pod and discard. Cut bacon into small pieces and place in a large serving bowl over hot water. Beat in eggs until frothy. Add cheese, salt and pepper. Mix well, then stir in butter. When spaghetti is *al dente* (firm, not too

soft), drain well and add bacon mixture. Toss well at table. Serve with additional grated cheese. Serves 4.

PIEDMONT GNOCCHI
(Potato Dumplings)

10 to 12 boiled potatoes, peeled
4 tablespoons butter or margarine
1 or 2 beaten eggs
½ tablespoon salt
½ teaspoon pepper
¼ teaspoon nutmeg

1¼ cups flour
½ cup cheese, grated
5 quarts boiling water seasoned with
   3 tablespoons salt
1 tablespoon butter
Mushroom or tomato sauce

Mash potatoes with butter. Add eggs, salt, pepper and nutmeg. Work flour into potatoes, kneading thoroughly. Add more flour if necessary. Cut "dough" into 4-inch squares. Roll into ropes ½ inch thick. Cut into 1-inch lengths. Cook no more than 15 at a time. Boil about 6 minutes. Gnocchi will rise to surface. Remove with strainer or slotted spoon. Keep water boiling. Repeat until all the gnocchi are cooked. Arrange in layers in baking dish. Sprinkle each layer with grated cheese. Top with dots of butter. Pop under broiler to brown. Many eat this piled high like spaghetti, covered with a thick mushroom or tomato sauce. Serves 2 as a main dish, 4 as a first course.

POTATO BLINTZES

1 egg yolk, beaten
¼ teaspoon salt
¼ teaspoon sugar
½ teaspoon melted butter
1½ cups milk
1 cup flour
1 egg white, stiffly beaten

Filling:
4 or 5 medium potatoes, peeled
½ cup onion, chopped
3 tablespoons meat drippings, fat
   or oil
5 tablespoons bouillon
⅛ teaspoon salt
¼ teaspoon pepper

Boil potatoes until tender. Meanwhile, beat egg yolk with salt, sugar, butter and milk. Add flour. Stir briskly until batter is smooth. Fold in egg white. Butter 6-inch skillet very lightly. Pour in very thin layer

JAYNE MANSFIELD

of batter — just enough to cover bottom of pan. Cook on one side only until golden brown. Turn on to wax paper. Repeat until batter is used up.

Prepare filling: Sauté onion in drippings. Mix in potatoes, mashing them in frying pan. Moisten with bouillon. Season with salt and pepper.

Spoon heaping tablespoons of filling onto the fried side of each blintz. Fold two sides into filling, fold one end over other. Fry in butter until brown. Serves 4 as a main dish.

GNOCCHI SEMOLINA

1½ cups quick-cooking farina	2 eggs, well beaten
1½ cups water	1½ cups cheese, grated
4 cups milk	6 tablespoons butter or margarine
3 teaspoons salt	4 tablespoons milk
Pinch of nutmeg	

Bring water and milk to boil. Add salt. Pour in farina, very gradually, to avoid lumps. Stir constantly over low heat until mixture is quite thick and smooth. Remove from heat. Stir in nutmeg, eggs and ½ cup grated cheese. Mix thoroughly. Pour onto lightly floured breadboard. Spread ½ inch thick. Cool. Cut into squares. Arrange in layers in shallow buttered casserole. Sprinkle each layer with 2 tablespoons grated cheese. Top with dots of butter. Sprinkle with milk. Bake in moderate (375°) oven 15 minutes. This can be prepared in advance. However, the baking should wait for the last minute. There is no fixed tradition about sauces: tomato, cheese or mushroom, as you like it.

SALMON CAVIAR

2 6-ounce salmon steaks	¼ teaspoon celery salt
¼ cup butter	Salt and pepper
2 tablespoons onion, finely chopped	2 tablespoons caviar
¼ cup dry white wine	2 egg yolks
1 cup heavy cream	

Arrange salmon steaks in heavy, buttered skillet. Add onion, wine, 4 tablespoons cream and celery salt. Season to taste. Cover. Simmer 10 minutes. Bone and skin salmon. Place in heated casserole. Heat liquid from skillet and add caviar. Reduce by one-third. Thicken with egg yolks which have been mixed with balance of cream. Pour over salmon. Serve at once. Serves 2.

TRUITES AMANDINES
(Trout with Almonds)

2 brook trout, about 1 pound each	6 tablespoons butter
Salt and pepper to taste	2 tablespoons almonds, blanched and
Cold milk	shredded
Flour	4 teaspoons lemon juice

Season trout with salt and pepper. Dip in milk. Roll in flour. Sauté over low heat in 3 tablespoons butter until brown on both sides. Remove. Keep hot. Add 3 tablespoons butter to pan. Heat till foaming. Stir in almonds. Cook about 1 minute. Shake pan constantly while cooking almonds. Sprinkle each fish with lemon juice. Pour the almond-butter mixture over each. Serves 2.

KENNEDY CLAM CHOWDER

2 dozen soft shell clams, shucked	Black pepper, freshly ground
2 ounces salt pork, diced	4 cups milk, scalded
2½ cups onion, sliced	2 cups light cream, scalded
6 cups potato, diced	3 tablespoons butter, blended with
2 small bay leaves, crumbled	2 tablespoons flour
1 tablespoon salt	

Strain clams. Reserve liquor. Mince hard part of clams. Chop soft part coarsely and reserve. Sauté pork until golden brown. Add minced clams, onion, potato, bay leaves, salt and pepper. Add 4 cups water. Bring to boil. Reduce heat. Cover. Simmer 15 minutes. Add clam liquor plus enough water to make 2 cups. Add chopped clams, milk, cream, and butter blended with flour. Simmer 20 minutes.

ZUCCHINI SOUFFLÉ

½ pound lamb, ground
1 onion, finely chopped
2 tablespoons butter
½ pound small zucchini, cubed
Dash pepper
1 teaspoon parsley, chopped
½ teaspoon salt
½ cup water
4 eggs
Tomato sauce

Brown lamb and onion in butter. Add zucchini, pepper, parsley, salt and water. Cook over low heat, stirring occasionally, until meat and vegetables are tender. Cool slightly. Stir in eggs. Pour into 1-quart soufflé dish. Bake in 375° oven 30 minutes. Cut into squares and serve hot with tomato sauce. Serves 2 to 3.

VEAL CHOPS ENVELOPPÉ

2 veal chops
3 tablespoons mushrooms, coarsely
       chopped and sautéed in butter
½ box piecrust mix
2 slices ham
1 egg yolk

Sauté chops quickly until brown without cooking through completely. Cool. Mix pastry as directed on box. Roll out 2 thin layers. Cut in 2 squares, each large enough to envelop one chop. Place a chop on each square and top with a spoonful of mushroom and a slice of ham. Fold the pastry around each, leaving bone sticking out. Brush with egg yolk. Cook in moderate (350°) oven about 30 minutes. Serve with Brown Sauce (see page 322). Before serving put paper frill on each bone. Serves 2.

BEEF PAGLIA

2 cups leftover roast beef
2 onions, sliced
¼ cup white vinegar
½ cup olive oil
4 tablespoons capers
2 tablespoons parsley, chopped

2 teaspoons tarragon, chopped
2 teaspoons chives, chopped
¼ teaspoon dry mustard
Tabasco sauce
Black pepper, freshly ground
Lettuce leaves

Cut roast beef to matchstick lengths. Separate onion slices into rings. Combine with beef, vinegar, oil, capers, herbs, mustard, a few drops of Tabasco, and pepper. Chill quickly in freezer for 20 minutes. Serve on crisp lettuce leaves. Serves 2.

QUICK CREAMED CHICKEN HASH

½ large green pepper, finely diced
2 cans concentrated cream of chicken
    soup
½ pint cream

3 cups cooked chicken, finely diced
1 teaspoon salt
½ teaspoon pepper, freshly ground

Simmer diced green pepper about 5 minutes in 1 cup of water. Drain. In a saucepan, thin the chicken soup slowly with cream over low heat. When sauce has reached the proper consistency, put in chicken, peppers and seasoning. Stir well, and continue to cook until hash is thoroughly hot. Serve on toast triangles or in patty shells. Garnish, if desired, with a few pinches of paprika. Serves 2.

CHICKEN POACHED IN CHAMPAGNE

1 roasting chicken, cut in pieces
Bacon fat
Oil
12 parboiled pearl onions
½ glass *marc de champagne* or
    grappa
½ glass brandy

½ bottle champagne
2 tablespoons flour
1 cup double cream
1 truffle, chopped
Salt
Pepper

Sauté chicken in fat and oil in heavy skillet until golden. Add onions. Set fire to heated *marc* and brandy. Spoon onto chicken. Add champagne. Season. Cook, covered, in oven 20 minutes. Remove chicken pieces. Skin. Keep warm. Put skillet on low burner and slowly add flour dissolved in cream. Stir till thickened. Add chopped truffle. Put in chicken pieces. Simmer a few minutes. Serve on rice.

CHICKEN LICKEN

1 cup avocado, diced	½ teaspoon salt
2 cups chicken bouillon, chilled	Black pepper, freshly ground
3 tablespoons lime juice	Tomato, diced

Mash avocado into chicken bouillon (or put both in electric blender). Stir in lime juice, salt and freshly ground pepper. Chill 20 minutes. Serve in chilled soup cups, garnished with diced tomato. Serves 2.

CHICKEN GRÉGOIRE

2 cups cooked or canned chicken fricassee
3 tablespoons Swiss cheese, grated
¼ cup light cream
1 teaspoon curry powder
½ bunch broccoli, cooked, or ½ package frozen broccoli

Heat chicken fricassee with cheese, cream and curry powder for 10 minutes, stirring frequently. Serve on hot platter, surrounded with broccoli. Serves 2.

CANDLELIGHT PEACHES

2 ripe peaches, peeled
8 wild strawberries
1 liqueur glass maraschino
Sugar

3 egg yolks
¼ bottle champagne
Rose petals

Sprinkle maraschino and sugar on peaches. Marinate with strawberries (*frais de bois* is what I mean — but you can cut up the large ones, if necessary) in refrigerator for several hours or in freezer for 30 minutes. Beat egg yolks and 2 tablespoons sugar in saucepan over low heat. Add champagne gradually. As soon as it begins to thicken, put in top of double boiler. Continue heating until thickened. Whisk over ice until cold. Serve peaches and strawberries in a glass dish. Add sauce. Decorate with rose petals, real or sugared. Serves 2.

FRANK MERRILL AND LILLIAN WORTH IN *Tarzan the Tiger*

BEEFCAKE

- BEEF AND PORK MEAT LOAF
- BEEFCAKE DAUBE
- BEEF POT ROAST
- BEEF PIE
- CURRIED BEEFCAKES AND RICE
- INDIVIDUAL BEEF PIES
- CHOPPED BEEF RING
- BEEFCAKES IN CRUST
- BAKED BEEFSTEAK WITH VEGE-TABLES
- PEPPER STEAK
- CREOLED HAMBURGERS
- CURRIED MEATBALLS AND RICE
- BEEF GOULASH

CHEESECAKE

- BEEFCAKE CHEESE BALLS
- CAMEMBERT CHEESE BALLS
- FLORENTINE CHEESE CASSEROLE
- CHEESE BRANDIED CHERRIES
- CHEESECAKE NEW YORK STYLE
- CHEESE AND WHITE WINE CASSE-ROLE
- QUICHE LORRAINE
- COTTAGE CHEESE CAKE
- PINEAPPLE CHEESE PIE
- COTTAGE CHEESE EGGS
- RASPBERRY CHEESECAKE
- GRAHAM CRACKER CHEESECAKE
- CHOCOLATE CHEESE PIE
- PARMESAN MOUSSE
- CUCUMBERS STUFFED WITH GOR-GONZOLA
- SWISS CHEESE SALAD

TRUTH compels me to admit that for most of us the human body, per se, is not always a thing of beauty and certainly never a joy forever. Those fortunate few who for some fleeting moments of their lives are lucky enough to approach the idealized proportions of what is considered beautiful, are instantly made into demigods and goddesses. Private lives are held up as examples of what or what not to do. Misfortunes, publicized as the height of hubris, give others comfort in the fact that they are less than perfect and perhaps luckier. Still, most of us would change places with any of them. We identify with them, and through them are able to slop along with what physical embodiments we are saddled with as one of the stops along the mutative road of genetics. It all adds up to sexual attraction and — leaving those few academicians aside — who does not want to be sexually attractive? But nature, contriving to control an overpopulated world, encourages us to reveal more and more. The bikini, having freed the navel, is traveling still further down. And as each inch is uncovered, each imperfection is revealed, thereby rendering it less useful for pleasurable purposes (witness the relative indifference of the hippies to nudity . . . they would rather be "stoned" than "laid," given the choice). Harking back to the perfect age when contrived nudity was titillation and not a lecture on anatomy seems like ancient history. I shudder to think of the future when all of the genitals will be revealed, opened, extended, and made the subject of the wide screen closeup — in glorious Technicolor, yet. No, no, I say, give me the days of the pin-up instead of the hang-up — the days of beefcake and cheesecake, when the reality was illusion and dreams were left to the imagination.

JOCK MAHONEY

BEEFCAKE

BEEF AND PORK MEAT LOAF

¾ pound ground veal
¾ pound ground pork
1 cup mushrooms, chopped
¼ cup fresh bread crumbs soaked in
 ½ cup white wine
1 egg, beaten
1 teaspoon salt

¼ teaspoon pepper
1 clove garlic, crushed
Nutmeg
1 cup sour cream
2 hard-boiled eggs, peeled
1 cup bouillon

Have meat ground twice through meat chopper. Mix meats with mushrooms, bread crumbs that have been soaked in white wine, beaten egg, salt, pepper, garlic, a good pinch of nutmeg and 4 tablespoons sour cream. When well mixed, form into loaf, molded around the hard-boiled eggs. Put remaining sour cream over meat loaf so that top and sides are well covered. Bake in preheated 400° oven ¾ hour, basting frequently. Remove meat loaf. Then add 1 cup boiling bouillon to bottom of dish and scrape whatever may be adhering to bottom and sides to use as a sauce.

BEEFCAKE DAUBE

3½ to 4 pounds beef shoulder roast
2 large cloves garlic, cut in slivers
1½ cups red wine
Salt and pepper
3 tablespoons bacon drippings
1 cup onion, sliced

1 tablespoon parsley, minced
1 bay leaf
¼ teaspoon thyme
½ cup green pepper, chopped
½ cup mushrooms, cut in pieces
1 cup boiling water

Make 4 or 5 slits in roast and insert garlic slivers. Marinate meat in wine, covered, 2½ to 3 hours. Turn several times. Remove meat. Reserve marinade. Sprinkle meat heavily with salt and pepper. Melt bacon grease in deep heavy skillet until bubbly. Sear roast until rich brown on all sides. Remove. Lightly brown onion in fat in which meat was seared. Add meat, parsley, bay leaf, thyme, green pepper, mushrooms, water and marinade. Bring to boil. Lower heat. Cover. Simmer until tender. Season sauce to taste with salt and pepper.

BEEF POT ROAST

3 pounds pot roast	3 onions, sliced
Salt and pepper	2 tablespoons tomato paste
2 tablespoons flour	2 cups water
4 tablespoons butter	1 bay leaf
¼ cup red wine	

Season meat with salt and pepper. Rub in flour. Brown meat in melted butter on all sides. Add wine and sliced onions. Cook until onions wilt. Add tomato paste, dissolved in water, and bay leaf. Cover. Simmer 3 hours. Serve with mashed potatoes or cooked rice.

NOTE: Diced carrots and celery may be added to this recipe.

BEEF PIE

3 pounds beef tenderloin, cut in cubes	1 bay leaf, crumbled
½ cup flour	1 tablespoon dry mustard
½ cup oil	2 teaspoons Worcestershire
2 cups onion, sliced	2 cups frozen peas
2 cloves garlic, crushed	½ recipe packaged pie crust
2 cans condensed consommé	1 teaspoon salt
1 cup water	Black pepper, freshly ground

Combine flour, salt and pepper in paper bag. Shake beef cubes in bag with flour mixture to coat thoroughly. Brown meat in oil in large saucepan. Remove meat. Add onion and garlic to remaining oil. Fry 10 minutes, stirring constantly. Add meat, consommé, water and seasonings. Bring to boil. Reduce heat. Cover and simmer for 1½ hours. Add peas. Pour into casserole. Top with pie crust, prepared as directed on package, rolled ⅛ inch thick. Bake in hot (425°) oven 30 minutes, until crust is brown.

CURRIED BEEFCAKES AND RICE

1 pound ground beef
2 teaspoons curry powder
1 cup packaged stuffing mix
1 beaten egg

½ cup butter
½ teaspoon salt
Black pepper, freshly ground

Mix beef, curry powder, stuffing mix, egg, salt and pepper together. Shape into small balls. Sauté in butter over high heat 5 minutes until brown. Pour over boiled rice.

INDIVIDUAL BEEF PIES

2 teaspoons salt
¼ teaspoon thyme
1 pound beef, cut in 1-inch cubes
2 tablespoons bacon drippings
2 cups boiling water
½ cup turnips, diced

½ cup carrots, diced
½ cup celery, diced
1 medium onion, sliced
2 tablespoons flour
Salt and pepper
Prepared biscuit mix

Mix salt and thyme. Rub into meat. Dredge in flour. Brown on all sides in hot drippings in a skillet. Transfer to saucepan. Add water and vegetables. Cook until meat is thoroughly tender. Thicken with flour dissolved in a small quantity of water. Pepper and salt to taste. Pour into individual casseroles. Roll out prepared biscuit dough to ¼-inch thickness. Cut to fit casseroles. Place dough over meat. Make 3 small slits in center of each piece of dough. Bake at 400° until brown.

CHOPPED BEEF RING

2 pounds lean beef, ground
¾ cup butter
½ cup onion, grated
2 cups soft bread crumbs
2½ generous teaspoons salt
2 teaspoons paprika
1½ teaspoons prepared mustard

Few grains cayenne
1 tablespoon parsley, finely chopped
1 tablespoon chives, finely chopped
⅔ cup tomato juice
⅓ cup tomato catsup
12 broiled tomato slices
1 tablespoon parsley, chopped

Mix beef, butter, grated onion, bread crumbs, salt, paprika, mustard, cayenne, parsley and chives. Put mixture through food chopper. Blend

KIRK DOUGLAS

thoroughly. Moisten with tomato juice. Pack into generously buttered ring mold. Spread tomato catsup over top. Bake in hot oven 45 minutes, until top is brown and meat shrinks from sides of ring mold. Unmold on heated platter. Fill center of ring with broiled tomato slices, garnished with parsley.

BEEFCAKES IN CRUST

1 pound ground chuck beef
½ pound ground fresh lean pork
½ pound liver sausage
1½ tablespoons onion, finely chopped
1½ tablespoons green celery leaves
1½ tablespoons parsley
1½ tablespoons green pepper
1½ tablespoons pimiento
1¼ teaspoons salt
½ teaspoon paprika
¼ teaspoon black pepper
⅓ cup stale bread crumbs soaked in ½ cup red wine
1 clove garlic, finely chopped
½ cup tomato catsup
¼ cup vinegar
2 teaspoons Worcestershire
½ clove garlic, crushed
1 tablespoon onion, grated
½ teaspoon chili powder
1 teaspoon prepared mustard
½ teaspoon salt
1 box pie crust mix, prepared as directed

Mix beef, pork and liver sausage. Add onion, celery leaves, parsley, green pepper and pimiento. Season with salt, paprika, black pepper, bread crumbs soaked in wine and garlic. Blend thoroughly. Shape mixture into 6 individual loaves 2 inches thick. Place in buttered shallow pan. Mix catsup, vinegar, Worcestershire, garlic, grated onion, chili powder and mustard. Add salt. Beat until well blended. Pour sauce evenly over meat loaves. Bake 35 minutes in moderate (350°) oven. Baste frequently. Cool loaves 10 minutes. Wrap each in flaky pie crust. Prick each dough with fork. Bake in hot (400°) oven 10 minutes. Brush loaves with melted butter. Bake 10 minutes longer. Serve hot or cold.

BAKED BEEFSTEAK WITH VEGETABLES

3½ pounds boneless sirloin steak 1¾ inches thick
1 cup dry gin
5 tablespoons butter
1 cup onion, sliced
1 cup green pepper cut in 1-inch pieces

1 cup celery, coarsely chopped
1 cup canned whole mushrooms
¼ cup butter
5 large tomatoes, cut in quarters
1 tablespoon parsley, minced
½ cup red wine
Salt and pepper

Marinate steak in gin several hours before cooking. Turn occasionally. Melt 3 tablespoons butter in shallow baking dish in 500° oven. Add steak. Allow 18 minutes for rare and 25 minutes for medium steak. Turn steak twice while cooking. Sauté onion, pepper, celery and mushrooms in ¼ cup melted butter over medium heat. Add tomatoes, parsley and wine. Season with salt and pepper. Cook over low heat. Stir gently from time to time. Five minutes before steak is done, sprinkle liberally on both sides with salt and pepper. Remove steak. Place on hot platter. Arrange tomato-mushroom mixture on top.

PEPPER STEAK

3 pounds very thinly sliced beef rump
3 green peppers, sliced
3 onions, sliced
1 clove garlic, crushed
9 large mushrooms, sliced
3 tomatoes, quartered

1 cup tomato purée
¾ cup butter
½ cup flour
1 cup red Burgundy
Salt
Black pepper, freshly ground

Make green pepper sauce: Sauté green peppers, onions, garlic, mushrooms and tomatoes in ½ cup butter 5 minutes. Add tomato purée. Simmer 10 minutes.

Salt and pepper meat. Dip in flour. Sauté in remaining butter 2 minutes. Add sauce. Simmer 15 minutes. Stir frequently. Add wine. Simmer 3 minutes.

BURT LANCASTER IN *Brute Force*

CREOLED HAMBURGERS

12 hamburgers
3 to 4 cups Creole Sauce

Prepare 6 individual hamburgers. Roll into balls, then flatten slightly. Have ready the Creole Sauce sizzling hot. Add prepared burgers. Cover tightly. Bake 25 to 30 minutes in moderate (375°) oven. Turn once during cooking.

CREOLE SAUCE

1 cup onion, chopped
2 tablespoons oil
1½ teaspoons salt
⅛ teaspoon pepper
1 cup celery, finely diced
1 can tomato soup
1 cup hot water

Sauté onion in oil. Add salt, pepper, celery, tomato soup and water. Cover and simmer about twenty minutes.

CURRIED MEATBALLS AND RICE

1 pound ground beef
2 teaspoons curry powder
1 tablespoon hot paprika
1 cup stuffing mix
½ teaspoon salt
Black pepper, freshly ground
½ cup butter

Mix beef, curry powder, paprika, stuffing mix, salt and pepper. Shape into 32 small balls. Sauté in butter over high heat 5 minutes or until brown. Good served with tomato sauce made with paprika.

BEEF GOULASH

3 pounds stewing beef, cubed
2 cups onion, chopped
½ cup butter
½ teaspoon marjoram
1½ teaspoons caraway seed
2 cloves garlic, minced
Salt

2 cups water
2 tablespoons paprika
1 tablespoon hot paprika
¼ cup catsup
2 tablespoons water
6 boiled potatoes
3 hard-cooked eggs, sliced

Sauté onion in butter 5 minutes. Add beef, marjoram, caraway, garlic, salt and 2 cups water. Bring to boil. Reduce heat. Cover. Simmer 1 hour. Combine paprika, catsup and 2 tablespoons water. Add this mixture to stew. Simmer 10 minutes. Serve with hot potatoes and sliced eggs.

CHEESECAKE

BEEFCAKE CHEESE BALLS

2 pounds lean sirloin steak, ground
1 onion, grated
1 teaspoon salt
1 teaspoon pepper
½ pound cream cheese
½ pound blue cheese
Egg, lightly beaten
Parsley, finely chopped

Combine raw ground steak with grated onion, salt and pepper. Blend together cream cheese and blue cheese. Form cheese mixture into tiny balls. Cover cheese balls with ground meat. Roll to make a double ball — cheese inside, meat outside. Dip meat-cheese balls in egg. Roll in parsley. Pierce each with cocktail pick. Makes about 50.

CAMEMBERT CHEESE BALLS

½ Camembert cheese
1 large Philadelphia cream cheese
2 tablespoons creamed butter
2¼ tablespoons flour
1 tablespoon rice flour
1 cup milk
Salt
Cayenne pepper
1 egg, beaten
Bread crumbs

Rub cheese through strainer. Add butter, flour, rice flour, milk, salt and cayenne pepper. Stir over low heat until thick. Pour onto a plate to cool. Form into small balls. Roll in flour. Brush with beaten egg. Roll in crumbs. Fry in deep fat until golden brown.

MARION DAVIES AND BILLIE DOVE IN *Blondie of the Follies*

FLORENTINE CHEESE CASSEROLE

8 ounces noodles
⅓ cup creamy cottage cheese
2 ounces cream cheese
¼ cup sour cream
1 frozen purée of spinach
¼ cup white wine
6 spring onions, finely chopped

1 teaspoon salt
½ teaspoon pepper
½ teaspoon nutmeg
2 tablespoons grated Parmesan
   cheese
2 tablespoons butter

Boil noodles in large quantity of salted water about 12 minutes. While noodles are boiling, mix cottage cheese with cream cheese, sour cream, spinach and white wine until almost smooth. Add onions, salt, pepper and nutmeg to cottage cheese mixture. Mix well. Drain noodles. Place noodles in a buttered casserole. Pour on cheese mixture. Stir well. Sprinkle grated Parmesan cheese over top. Dot with butter. Place casserole in a preheated moderate (350°) oven. Bake 30 minutes. Serve hot.

CHEESE BRANDIED CHERRIES

1 pound cottage cheese
2½ cups canned Bing cherries plus
   juice
¾ cup brandy
1 cup heavy cream
1 teaspoon salt

Press cottage cheese through coarse sieve. Line strainer with cheese-cloth. Put cheese in strainer and set in bowl. Refrigerate overnight or for at least 8 hours to drain. Combine brandy with cherries and juice. Bring to boil. Stir occasionally. Remove from heat. Cover. Chill at least 1 hour. Whip cream with salt until stiff. Mix whipped cream with drained cottage cheese. Stir lightly until mixed. Serve cheese and cream mixture on platter surrounded by chilled brandied cherries.

BETTY FURNESS

CHEESECAKE, NEW YORK STYLE

1 box pie crust mix	¼ teaspoon salt
2½ pounds cream cheese	1 teaspoon vanilla extract
1¾ cups sugar	6 eggs
2 tablespoons flour	½ cup heavy cream

Prepare dough for two 9-inch pie crusts, as directed on package. Wrap in waxed paper. Place in refrigerator for 1 hour. Preheat oven to 400°. Roll out ⅓ of dough on lightly floured board to form 9-inch circle. Place on bottom of 9-inch spring-form pan. Bake in 400° oven 10 minutes. Remove from oven. Butter sides of spring form. Fasten it in place over base. Roll remaining dough in long strips to fit sides and press into place, joining bottom edges. Preheat oven to 475°.

Now prepare filling: Beat cheese with rotary beater until light and fluffy. Add sugar, flour, salt and vanilla gradually. Beat constantly. Add eggs, one at a time. Beat after each addition. Add cream. Blend well.

Pour into prepared pan. Bake at 475° 10 minutes. Then reduce temperature to 225° and bake 1 hour. Turn off oven. Open door. Do not remove cake for 5 minutes. Then set to cool in draft-free place for about 2 to 3 hours.

CHEESE AND WHITE WINE CASSEROLE

6 slices stale bread	¾ teaspoon salt
Garlic butter (4 tablespoons butter kneaded with 1 clove crushed garlic)	½ teaspoon prepared mustard
	½ teaspoon paprika
	Few grains cayenne
3 eggs, beaten lightly	1 teaspoon Worcestershire
1 cup dry white wine	2 cups grated Swiss cheese
½ cup chicken bouillon	

Trim bread slices. Spread with garlic butter. Cut in strips. Line sides and bottom of shallow earthenware casserole with strips, buttered side down. Mix beaten eggs lightly with wine and chicken bouillon. Season with salt, mustard, paprika and cayenne. Add Worcestershire. Beat in cheese very slowly. Pour over bread in casserole. Bake in moderate (325°) oven 30 minutes.

ROCHELLE HUDSON

QUICHE LORRAINE

6 rather thick slices bacon,
cut in half
½ box pie crust mix
12 thin slices Swiss cheese, cut in
pieces 1 inch wide
4 eggs

1 tablespoon flour
Generous grating nutmeg
½ teaspoon salt
Few grains cayenne
2 cups light cream
1¼ tablespoons butter, melted

Broil bacon. Drain on absorbent paper. Prepare pie crust mix as directed on box. Line 9-inch pie plate with pie crust. Cover bottom of pie crust with overlapping layers of cheese and bacon. Beat eggs together with flour, nutmeg, salt and cayenne. Add light cream. Stir in melted butter. Strain over bacon and cheese. Bake the *quiche* in moderate (375°) oven about 40 minutes, until set and top nicely browned. Serve warm.

COTTAGE CHEESE CAKE

18 slices zwieback, rolled into fine
crumbs
¼ cup melted butter
1 tablespoon sugar
1 pound creamy cottage cheese
¼ cup sifted flour
4 egg yolks

1 cup sugar
Juice of ½ lemon
1½ teaspoons grated lemon rind
½ teaspoon vanilla
Pinch salt
1 cup heavy cream, whipped
4 egg whites, beaten stiff

Mix zwieback crumbs with melted butter and 1 tablespoon sugar. Press ¾ of zwieback crust mixture onto the bottom and sides of well-buttered 9-inch spring-form pan. Force cottage cheese through sieve. Mix it with flour. Beat thoroughly until light and fluffy. Beat egg yolks until light. Gradually add ½ cup sugar. Beat until thick and pale. Add lemon juice, grated lemon rind, vanilla and salt. Fold into cottage cheese. Fold in whipped cream and egg whites with remaining sugar. Blend well. Turn into zwieback crust. Sprinkle top with remaining crumbs. Bake in a slow (300°) oven 1 hour. Turn off heat. Open door. Cool cake an hour in oven. Cool thoroughly before removing from pan.

LUPE VELEZ

PINEAPPLE CHEESE PIE

½ pound creamy cottage cheese
1 cup sugar
¼ cup butter, softened
½ cup flour
½ teaspoon salt
2 eggs

¾ cup milk scalded with 1 teaspoon vanilla
2½ cups crushed pineapple
1 tablespoon cornstarch
½ box pie crust mix

Prepare crust for one 9-inch pie shell. Rub cottage cheese through fine sieve with sugar. Mix thoroughly. Add softened butter. Beat until light. Sift flour with salt. Blend into cheese mixture. Add eggs, one at a time, alternately with cooled milk. Beat well after each addition. Heat pineapple. Stir in cornstarch diluted with a little cold water. Cook 1 minute, stirring constantly. Cool pineapple mixture. Turn into unbaked pie shell. Pour cheese mixture over fruit. Bake in hot (400°) oven 10 minutes. Reduce temperature to moderate (350°). Bake 30 minutes longer — until cheese is set. Cool. Chill in refrigerator.

COTTAGE CHEESE EGGS

½ pound dried beef, cut in thin strips
8 tablespoons scallions, finely minced
4 tablespoons butter
1 cup cottage cheese

12 eggs, well beaten
6 toasted English muffins, cut in half
Paprika
Watercress

Sauté beef and scallions in butter. Stir constantly until scallions are lightly browned. Remove from direct heat and set over hot water. Meanwhile: Beat cottage cheese with eggs until very smooth. Pour mixture over beef and onions. Cook over hot water pan, stirring frequently, until thick but still soft. Serve on toasted English muffins. Sprinkle with paprika. Garnish with watercress.

BETTY GRABLE IN *The Dolly Sisters*

RASPBERRY CHEESECAKE

⅓ cup butter
⅓ cup sugar
2 eggs
¾ cup milk
1½ cups flour
1 tablespoon baking powder
2 cups raspberries, fresh

1 3-ounce package cream cheese
2 tablespoons sugar
1 tablespoon lemon juice
1 cup flour
¼ cup sugar
¼ cup butter
¼ teaspoon cinnamon

Preheat oven to 375°. Cream butter and sugar until fluffy. Add eggs. Beat well. Add milk and flour mixed with baking powder. Add half the raspberries. Mix thoroughly. Pour into buttered 9-inch cake pan. Top with remaining berries. Combine cream cheese, sugar and lemon juice. Spread over berries. Combine flour, sugar, butter and cinnamon. Mix until crumbly. Sprinkle over all. Bake 30 minutes.

GRAHAM CRACKER CHEESECAKE

1¼ cups graham cracker crumbs
¼ cup melted butter
2 teaspoons brown sugar
2 8-ounce packages cream cheese
1 teaspoon vanilla

1 teaspoon lemon extract
¾ cup granulated sugar
3 eggs
1 pint sour cream

Preheat oven to 375°. Mix graham cracker crumbs with butter and brown sugar. Press on bottom of buttered 9-inch spring-form pan. Blend cheese until smooth and fluffy in electric mixer. Add ½ teaspoon vanilla and ½ teaspoon lemon extract and ½ cup granulated sugar. Blend in eggs. Mix thoroughly. Pour into prepared pan. Bake 20 minutes. Remove. Set aside for 20 minutes. Raise oven temperature to 475°. Mix sour cream with remaining vanilla, lemon extract and sugar. Spread evenly over cheesecake. Bake 10 minutes longer. Cool.

GINGER ROGERS

CHOCOLATE CHEESE PIE

1¼ cups graham cracker crumbs
1 tablespoon light brown sugar
⅛ teaspoon nutmeg
¼ cup melted butter
1 cup semi-sweet chocolate pieces
8 ounces cream cheese

¾ cup brown sugar
⅛ teaspoon salt
2 eggs, separated
1 cup whipped cream
1 teaspoon vanilla

Mix crumbled graham crackers with brown sugar and nutmeg and melted butter. Butter 9-inch spring-form pan. Press crumbs on bottom. Chill in refrigerator. Prepare filling: Melt chocolate over hot water. Blend cream cheese in bowl with ½ cup brown sugar and salt. Beat in egg yolks. Stir in melted chocolate. Beat egg whites until stiff. Gradually beat remaining brown sugar into egg whites. Fold into chocolate mixture. Fold in whipped cream and vanilla. Pour into graham cracker crust. Chill overnight.

PARMESAN MOUSSE

¼ cup butter
½ cup flour
1¼ cups milk
⅔ cup grated Parmesan cheese
½ small onion, minced
1 teaspoon dry mustard
Salt, pepper, paprika to taste

2 envelopes gelatin
½ cup chicken stock
4 eggs, separated
¼ cup whipped cream
½ cup chives, chopped
Parsley

Melt butter. Stir in flour. Cook over low heat, stirring constantly, 3 minutes. Add milk gradually. Cook, stirring with whisk, until it is thick and smooth. Add cheese, onion, mustard, salt, pepper and paprika. Soften gelatin in chicken stock. Dissolve in white sauce. Remove from heat. Beat in egg yolks, one at a time. Cool mixture. Fold in stiffly beaten egg whites and whipped cream. Sprinkle a lightly oiled 2-quart mold with chopped chives. Pour in cheese mixture. Be careful to keep chives on lining of mold. Chill 3 hours. Unmold on serving platter. Surround with ring of parsley.

ANN SHERIDAN

CUCUMBERS STUFFED WITH GORGONZOLA

3 cucumbers
3 tablespoons Gorgonzola cheese
3 tablespoons softened butter
1 tablespoon cognac
2 tablespoons chives, chopped

Peel cucumbers with fluted vegetable knife. Cut into 1-inch slices. Remove seedy center from each slice to form tiny cups. Cream together Gorgonzola cheese and butter. Moisten mixture with cognac. Fill cucumber cups with cheese mixture. Sprinkle with chopped chives. Serve on white toast cut the same size.

SWISS CHEESE SALAD

½ cup thick sour cream
1½ teaspoons dry mustard
1 teaspoon grated horseradish
Pinch ground cumin seed
½ teaspoon salt

½ teaspoon pepper
½ pound Swiss cheese, cut into 1-inch sticks
6 hard-cooked eggs, finely chopped
Salad greens

Mix sour cream with mustard, horseradish, cumin seed, salt and pepper. Toss cheese sticks lightly with eggs. Arrange on crisp salad greens tossed with sour cream dressing.

JOANNE WOODWARD IN *The Stripper*

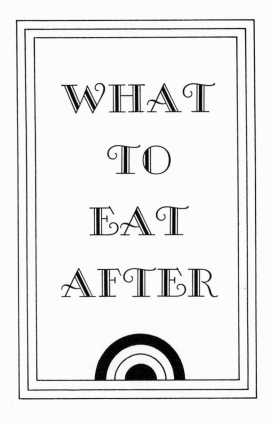

WHAT
TO
EAT
AFTER

SCENE FROM *Sodom and Gomorrah*

- GANGBANG HAM WITH PORT SAUCE
- GANGBANG CHICKEN TETRAZZINI
- PORK CHOPS WITH SAUERKRAUT
- GANGBANG LASAGNE
- WINE MEAT LOAF
- INDIAN VEAL STEW
- CHICKEN AND MUSHROOM PAR-TOUSE
- GANGBANG COUSCOUS
- GANGBANG ARROZ CON POLLO
- GANGBANG RIJSTAFFEL CURRY
- GANGBANG GUMBO
- GANGBANG CRAB GUMBO
- CORNED BEEF AND CABBAGE
- GANGBANG CHEESE SOUFFLÉ
- MULLIGATAWNY SOUP
- GANGBANG BEEF IN RED WINE
- CHILI CON CARNE
- QUICK GANGBANG CHILI
- GANGBANG MEXICAN BEEF WITH OLIVES
- GANGBANG MEXICAN CHICKEN
- GANGBANG IRISH STEW
- BARBECUED BONED "COUNTRY STYLE" SPARERIBS
- MEXICAN CHICKEN CASSEROLE
- LOVERS LAMB STEW
- GANGBANG PAELLA (VALENCIA STYLE)

Twenty men? Not even my idlest daydreams of Myra Breckinridge, warrior queen, ever included a scene in which I was called upon to master twenty men at the same time. Might it not be too much, psychologically?

— *Myra Breckinridge,* CHAPTER 19

Perhaps I might just . . . *watch,* you know and perhaps help out, in little ways . . .

— CHAPTER 19

. . . a tickle here, a pull there, a lick, a bite, no more. . . . The party ended in an orgy of eating. Delicate girls devoured cold cuts as though they had not been fed in weeks, while spent youths lay snoring among tangled towels that smelled of new-made love.

— CHAPTER 20

SUCCESSFUL entertaining on a grand scale is the deciding factor between a great host and your ordinary cockamamie cook. Provide an evening of fun and games for twenty people, having them leave fully satisfied and properly fed, and you're in. Your reputation will soar, the invitations will come pouring in, the phone will never stop ringing. Yet, you must remember, it takes a lot of effort and planning — but then, nothing that is easy comes good. The guests must be chosen with care and forethought. At the least, they must be congenial and have more in common than not. What will each one's contribution be — will he or she sit like a wallflower just watching, or will each help out, in his own way?

The good sport is always welcome while the greedy and aggressive, who grab anything in sight, or the bores who end up with their hands in their pockets, so to speak, must be avoided at all costs. Once the guest list is arrived at, the careful host will then give thought to the table settings, linens, lighting effects (now don't forget the guest towels), how to amuse your guests and loosen them up before the food arrives, and finally, what to eat. I prefer something hot because it shows that you have cared enough to give of yourself. Anybody can order up a ham and turkey from the corner delicatessen, but how many care enough to go to the trouble of making a chicken tetrazzini, or chili con carne. Dishes like these can be kept cooking or simmering while you play gracious host. Of course, you may have to disappear into the kitchen once or twice during the evening to check or baste, but I've found that upon returning it's always possible to take up where you left off — and with a largish group, you will not be missed that much. Indeed, sometimes I have been disheartened to realize that I had not been missed at all. In such moments, I take comfort in the thought that it is the successful mother whose children are able to leave home and survive independently.

So like a good mother-host, give your guests a sense of direction, never forcing. Set a good example by just being there when the need arises — and it almost always does. You'll find that your true compensation comes later on when, as the time approaches for the buffet, served hot and beautifully, your guests will be as pleased that they are there as you are that they have come.

GANGBANG HAM WITH PORT SAUCE

12 pounds tenderized ham
40 cloves
1 quart water
2 cups white wine
1 small stick cinnamon

2 medium-sized apples, quartered
1 orange, cut in pieces
1 cup crushed pineapple
1 pound brown sugar

Remove excess fat from ham. Score with cooky cutter or knife, making squares. In each square place a clove. Set in roaster. Add water, wine, cinnamon, apples, orange and pineapple with juices. Bake at 300° 2 hours, basting every 20 minutes. Sprinkle brown sugar on top of ham. Bake 1 hour longer, basting every 10 minutes to glaze ham evenly. If liquid reduces too fast during baking, keep adding hot water. When ham is cooked, liquid should be reduced to a heavy syrup. Serve with Port Sauce. Serves 16 to 18.

PORT SAUCE

1 cup port
Juice and peel of 1 medium orange,
    peel cut into matchstick lengths
3 tablespoons plum jelly
1 medium bay leaf
⅛ teaspoon coriander
3 cups drippings
Salt
2 teaspoons cornstarch

Heat port, orange juice and peel in skillet. Reduce to half. Add jelly, bay leaf, coriander and drippings. Reduce again. Remove bay leaf. Salt to taste. Thicken with cold cornstarch that has been mixed with a little port.

GANGBANG CHICKEN TETRAZZINI

6 2-pound chickens, cut up
2 cups celery tops, chopped
¾ cup parsley, chopped
3 small onions, sliced
2½ teaspoons salt
2½ pounds mushrooms, sliced
½ cup butter
4 tablespoons flour
Black pepper, freshly ground

½ teaspoon grated nutmeg
3 cups heavy cream
2 cups Parmesan cheese, grated
½ cup dry sherry
1½ pounds fine noodles, boiled and drained
1½ cups dry bread crumbs
Truffles

Place chickens in saucepan with celery, parsley, onions and 2 teaspoons salt. Add 3 cups water. Bring to boil. Cover. Reduce heat. Simmer for 30 minutes. Remove chickens and bone them. Strain broth and keep it.

Sauté mushrooms in butter. Stir in flour, ½ teaspoon salt, pepper and nutmeg. Slowly add 2 cups broth and the cream. Cook, stirring constantly, until thickened. Add half the Parmesan. Add chicken and sherry to sauce.

Mix half the chicken mixture with the hot noodles. Place noodles in greased, shallow baking dish. Top with remaining chicken mixture. Sprinkle with bread crumbs and 1 cup cheese. Dot with butter. Brown in broiler. Serve garnished with as many thinly sliced white truffles as you can afford. Serves 16 to 18.

Prepare early in the day — reheat — and brown just before serving.

PORK CHOPS WITH SAUERKRAUT

16 to 18 pork chops, center cut, boned
6 pounds sauerkraut
4 tablespoons tomato paste

3 tablespoons sweet paprika
3 tablespoons caraway seeds
6 cups water
Salt and pepper to taste

In skillet brown pork chops well. Put sauerkraut in a casserole. When chops are brown, drain drippings into sauerkraut. Add tomato paste, paprika and caraway seeds. Place chops on top of sauerkraut and add water, salt and pepper. Cover. Simmer about 1 hour until chops are very tender. This casserole may be baked in the oven early in the day, if desired. Serves 16 to 18.

GANGBANG LASAGNE

2 pounds lasagne, boiled and drained
2 cups onion, chopped
1 cup olive oil
5 tablespoons butter
4 cloves garlic, crushed
3½ pounds beef, ground
1½ teaspoons ground allspice
¾ teaspoon red pepper, crushed
1½ teaspoons salt

Black pepper, freshly ground
1½ cups tomato sauce
3 cups Parmesan cheese, grated

For Béchamel:
  5 tablespoons flour
  5 tablespoons butter
  5 cups milk
  2 cups Parmesan cheese

Sauté onion in olive oil and 4 tablespoons butter 10 minutes. Add garlic. Sauté 5 minutes. Add beef. Sauté 15 minutes, stirring frequently. Add spices. Cover and simmer for 15 minutes, stirring frequently.

Make Béchamel Sauce: In a saucepan stir 5 tablespoons flour into 5 tablespoons melted butter. Mix thoroughly. Gradually stir in 5 cups milk. Stir until thickened. Add 2 cups Parmesan cheese.

Pour about ¼ inch tomato sauce in bottom of baking dish. Put 1 layer of lasagne on top of sauce, add ⅓ Béchamel and ⅓ of meat mixture. Sprinkle lightly with Parmesan. Repeat, ending with a layer of lasagne. Pour about 1 cup of tomato sauce over the lasagne. Bake in moderate (375°) oven 30 minutes. Serves 16 to 18.

Prepare early in the day.

WINE MEAT LOAF

1 pound lean veal
1 pound lean ham
1 pound fresh lean pork
½ pound lean round steak
½ pound calf's liver with skin removed
½ teaspoon ground bay leaves
4 peppercorns, freshly ground
⅛ teaspoon mace
⅛ teaspoon sage
⅛ teaspoon thyme
⅛ teaspoon allspice
1 clove garlic, finely chopped
2 teaspoons shallots or onion, finely chopped

Parsley
2 teaspoons chives
Salt
1 cup rich beef bouillon
½ cup Madeira
2 teaspoons Worcestershire sauce
Few grains chili powder or cayenne
½ cup butter
Flaky pastry crust
½ cup cooked smoked tongue, coarsely chopped
½ cup cold cooked calf's liver, cut into small cubes
About ½ cup red port

Put veal, ham, pork, round steak and calf's liver through meat grinder, using finest blade. Combine ground meat in mixing bowl with bay leaves, peppercorns, mace, sage, thyme, allspice, garlic, shallots or onion, parsley, chives and salt to taste. Reduce 1 cup bouillon to ½ cup over high heat and add it to meat mixture with Madeira, Worcestershire sauce and a few grains of chili powder or cayenne. Blend thoroughly, cover with a cloth, and let meat stand for at least 4 hours in a cool place, but not in the refrigerator.

Heat butter in a large skillet and stir in meat mixture. With an asbestos pad under the skillet, cook gently for 30 minutes, stirring frequently to prevent scorching. Add salt if necessary.

Grease a large bread loaf pan and line with flaky pastry crust. Pour ⅓ of meat mixture into pan and sprinkle with tongue. Over this place another third of meat mixture. Sprinkle with ½ cup cold calf's liver and cover with remaining meat. Adjust top crust, sealing it carefully at edges, and prick pastry with fork. Bake in hot oven on baking sheet for 15 minutes. Lower heat to moderate and bake for 45 minutes longer, placing buttered paper over top if crust browns too fast. While loaf is still hot, place paper funnel in a hole in the center and fill loaf with as much red port as it will absorb, probably about ½ cup. Invert pan to slice and serve hot or cold.

INDIAN VEAL STEW

½ cup butter
8 pounds veal shoulder meat, cubed
6 tablespoons flour
2 onions, chopped
2 apples, chopped
2 bananas, chopped
4 ounces unsweetened coconut, chopped
4 tablespoons plumped raisins
2 tomatoes, chopped

6 whole cloves
¼ teaspoon thyme
2 bay leaves
8 teaspoons curry powder
1 teaspoon cardamon
1 teaspoon turmeric
2 quarts water
Salt to taste
2 pints heavy cream

Melt butter in a deep pan. Add meat. Cook slowly on low heat about 5 minutes. Do not brown. Stir in flour. Mix carefully with wooden spoon. Add onion, apple, banana, coconut, raisins, tomatoes, cloves, thyme, bay leaves, curry powder, cardamon, turmeric, water and salt to taste. Cook slowly, stirring constantly, until boiling. Cover. Simmer slowly about 1 hour and 15 minutes. Remove meat from sauce. Place on heated serving platter.

Add heavy cream to sauce. Simmer for 15 minutes. Pour over meat and serve very hot. Serves 20.

CHICKEN AND MUSHROOM PARTOUSE

36 pieces chicken (breasts, thighs or drumsticks)
Salt, pepper and paprika
¾ cup butter or margarine
¾ pound fresh mushrooms, sliced

4 tablespoons (¼ cup) flour
1½ cups chicken broth
6 tablespoons sherry
3 sprigs fresh rosemary or ½ teaspoon crumbled dried rosemary

Sprinkle chicken with salt, pepper and paprika. Brown in half the butter. Remove to an ovenproof casserole. Add remaining butter to drippings. Sauté sliced mushrooms until tender. Sprinkle flour over mushrooms. Stir in chicken broth, sherry and rosemary. Simmer until thickened, then pour over chicken. Cover. Bake in moderate (350°) oven 45 minutes. Makes 16 to 18 servings.

GANGBANG COUSCOUS

6 small stewing chickens, disjointed
6 pounds lamb, cut in squares
1½ pounds butter
12 onions, chopped
Chicken broth to cover
12 carrots, sliced
12 tomatoes, chopped
6 green peppers, cut in small squares
Salt and pepper

¾ teaspoon cayenne pepper to taste
7 cups couscous or wheat semolina or cracked wheat
7 cups cold salted water
7 cups canned chick-peas, drained
3 packages frozen green peas
6 cups zucchini, cut in thick pieces
18 fresh or frozen artichoke hearts
1 cup butter

Brown chicken and lamb in deep pan in ¾ cup butter with onions. Add just enough chicken broth to cover, and carrots, tomatoes, green peppers, salt, pepper and cayenne pepper — more or less according to taste. Bring to slow boil. Meanwhile, add couscous, wheat semolina or cracked wheat to salted water. (Rub well between fingers above bowl). Allow couscous to fall slowly into water, rubbing well. Do not allow lumps to form. Repeat until all water is absorbed. Place couscous in a cheesecloth in a colander or strainer over broth containing chicken

and lamb. Cover the deep pan tightly with aluminum foil and a pot cover. Cook 1 hour. Add chick-peas, green peas, zucchini and artichoke hearts to meat mixture. Replace colander and cover. Continue cooking for 1 hour until meats and couscous are tender. Stir 4 tablespoons butter into couscous. Serve couscous surrounded by vegetables and meat with broth on the side. Serves 18 to 20.

GANGBANG ARROZ CON POLLO

½ cup olive oil
6 cloves garlic, crushed
4 large onions, chopped
4 sweet red peppers, cut in squares
2 3-pound chickens, cut in small pieces
1 pound lean boiled ham, diced
2 pounds shrimp, cooked and shelled
2 Number 2 cans peeled tomatoes
2 packages frozen artichoke hearts

2 small packets saffron
2 cups chicken broth
2 bay leaves
Salt and pepper
2 packages frozen peas
4 cups rice, uncooked
Lobster tails, mussels, fish fillets (optional)
Strips of pimiento

Heat olive oil in heavy saucepan. Add garlic, onions, sweet red peppers. Cook until onions are soft. Add chicken and ham. Cook until golden brown. Stir in shrimp, peeled tomatoes, artichoke hearts, saffron dissolved in chicken broth, bay leaves, salt and pepper. Cover tightly and cook slowly until chicken is tender — about 45 minutes. Add peas 15 minutes before serving. Cook rice according to package directions. Drain. Mix with chicken and vegetables. Lobster tails, mussels, fish fillets may be cooked separately and added when serving. Garnish with strips of pimiento. Serves 18 to 20.

GANGBANG RIJSTAFFEL CURRY

4 chickens, cut up
Seasoned flour
¾ cup butter
9 large onions, minced
6 cloves garlic, crushed
6 tablespoons butter
6 tablespoons curry powder
3 teaspoons chili powder
¾ teaspoon cinnamon
1½ teaspoons ground ginger
2 quarts chicken stock

1 Number 2 can tomatoes
½ cup chutney, finely chopped
1½ cups seedless raisins
Salt and pepper
1½ cups almonds, blanched and slivered
3 tablespoons butter
1½ cups milk or cream
3 cups diced cucumber
Juice of 2 lemons

CONDIMENTS

Mango chutney, both mild and hot
Diced hard-boiled egg white
Diced hard-boiled egg yolk
Shredded hard-toasted fish fillets
Shredded crisp fried bacon
Minced mild onions
Grated lemon peel
Grated orange or grapefruit peel

Minced sweet pepper
Shredded fresh extra-ripe pineapple
Chopped mixed nuts
Plump raisins
Bananas fried in cinnamon and butter
Diced fried eggplant
Peeled diced cucumber
Diced candied ginger

Dredge chicken in seasoned flour. Brown in butter. Remove. Brown onions and garlic in same pan, adding butter. Add curry powder, chili powder, cinnamon and ginger. Stir in chicken stock, tomatoes, chutney, raisins, salt and pepper to taste. Add chicken. Cover. Simmer gently 1 hour. Remove chicken from bones. Cut in small pieces. Meanwhile, fry almonds until brown in butter. Put in blender with milk or cream. Add to chicken with cucumber. Simmer very slowly another ½ hour until thick. If too dry, add more chicken stock. Just before serving, add lemon juice. Serve in chafing dish surrounded by rice and condiments.

GANGBANG GUMBO

2 pounds peeled shrimp
4 quarts water
6 white onions, chopped
2 tablespoons flour
2 tablespoons shortening
8 green onions, chopped
2 bell peppers, chopped
3 bay leaves, crushed
2 cups celery, chopped
2 pounds tomatoes, peeled

2 pounds crab meat
1½ cups raw ham, cut in chunks
3 dozen oysters
1 teaspoon thyme
2 teaspoons salt
½ teaspoon pepper
3 cups cut okra
2 tablespoons gumbo filé
4 cups rice
½ cup parsley, chopped

Boil shrimp in water with 2 onions 15 minutes. Strain shrimp. Reserve water. Brown flour in shortening. Add remaining 4 white onions, green onions and bell peppers, bay leaves and celery. Cook 10 minutes. Add tomatoes and cook for 3 minutes. Add shrimp water. Cook 20 minutes. Add crab meat, ham, oysters, cooked shrimp, thyme, salt, pepper and okra. Cook 20 minutes. Add gumbo filé at the last minute. Stir. Turn off heat. Serve with boiled rice mixed with the parsley. Serves 16 to 20.

NOTE: Never reheat after addition of filé.

GANGBANG CRAB GUMBO

¾ cup butter
1½ cups onion, chopped
1 cup green peppers, chopped
1½ cups lean raw ham, cut in chunks
3 cups raw okra, sliced
3 cups tomato juice
1½ cups raw shelled deveined shrimp
1½ pounds crab meat

1½ quarts chicken stock
1 bay leaf
1 teaspoon basil
½ teaspoon thyme
½ cup parsley, minced
Salt and cayenne pepper to taste
1 cup bourbon
1 teaspoon gumbo filé (optional)
Steamed rice

Brown onion, pepper, ham and okra in melted butter. Add tomato juice, shrimp, crab meat, boiling stock, bay leaf, basil, thyme, parsley, salt and cayenne. Bring to boil. Lower heat. Simmer in covered pan 20 minutes. Add bourbon. Cook 3 minutes. Remove from heat. Stir in filé powder, if desired. Serve with rice. Serves 18 to 20.

NOTE: Never reheat gumbo after filé powder is added.

CORNED BEEF AND CABBAGE

8 pounds brisket corned beef
16 potatoes, cut in half
16 small white turnips
12 small carrots
12 small onions

3 large cabbages, cut into wedges
Butter
3 cups horseradish, grated
Mustard pickles

Soak corned beef in cold water for 1 hour. Drain. Cover with fresh, cold water. Bring slowly to boil. Skim frequently. Simmer very gently for about 4 hours (do not let it actually boil; it toughens the meat). 30 minutes before beef is done, add onions, carrots and turnips. Cook until tender. Boil potatoes in another pan. Boil cabbage separately for about 15 to 18 minutes. When tender, lift meat onto a large platter; rub with butter. Slice thin. Allow 2 slices for each portion. Garnish platter with potatoes, carrots, turnips, onions and cabbage. Serve with freshly grated horseradish and mustard pickles.

SCENE FROM *Cleopatra*

GANGBANG CHEESE SOUFFLÉ

1½ quarts milk
3 tablespoons salt
1¾ cups quick-cooking tapioca
2 pounds cheese, grated
15 eggs, separated

Scald milk. Add salt and tapioca and cook over water for 30 minutes. Add cheese and well-beaten egg yolks. Beat egg whites until stiff and fold in. Pour into large, oiled baking pans (12″ x 18″), or as many casseroles as required. Bake at 300° for 1 hour. Serve immediately. Serves 20 to 25.

MULLIGATAWNY SOUP

10 pounds chicken parts
9 cups water
4 cups carrots, sliced
1 cup onion, chopped
4 cups celery, chopped
½ cup parsley flakes
2 cups mushrooms, chopped
⅛ teaspoon Tabasco
½ cup onion, minced
6 tablespoons shortening
6 tablespoons flour
6 tablespoons curry powder
4 teaspoons salt
1½ cups heavy cream
3 quarts cooked rice

Combine first 8 ingredients. Cover. Cook until chicken is tender, approximately 1 hour. Bone and cut up chicken and return meat to stock. Brown onion in shortening. Stir in flour, curry powder and salt. Gradually add chicken stock. Cook 10 minutes. Stir in heavy cream. Heat thoroughly (do not boil). Serve with rice. Serves 16 to 18.

GANGBANG BEEF IN RED WINE

6 pounds rump of beef
4 tablespoons butter, melted
8 cups canned tomatoes
8 medium onions, sliced
6 carrots, sliced
2 stalks celery
5 cups red wine
4 cloves garlic, halved
1 teaspoon whole black peppercorns
¼ teaspoon thyme
2 bay leaves
Salt to taste
About 1¼ quarts beef broth

Brown meat on all sides in melted butter in skillet. Transfer meat to a rack in covered roaster or Dutch oven. Add tomatoes, onions, carrots, celery, wine and seasonings. Add broth to cover meat.

Roast at 350° for about 2½ hours, until meat is tender. Remove meat to a hot platter and strain broth. Serve broth hot with meat. Serves 16 to 18.

CHILI CON CARNE

3 cups red beans, dried, or
    4 Number 2 cans chili beans
	5 pounds lean beef, cut in ¼-inch
	    cubes

4 tablespoons salad or olive oil	3 tablespoons flour
3 onions, chopped	4 Number 2 cans tomatoes
6 tablespoons chili powder	4 to 6 drops Tabasco (optional)
4 cloves garlic, minced	2 tablespoons salt

If dried beans are used, wash carefully and discard any imperfect ones. Place in saucepan with water to cover and soak overnight. Wash thoroughly again and cover beans with fresh water. Cook over low heat until beans are tender, about 3 hours. Drain well.

Heat oil in separate saucepan and add onions, chili powder, garlic and beef. Cook over high heat until meat is very brown on all sides. Reduce heat to low. Add flour. Stir constantly until well blended. Add tomatoes and Tabasco. Cover and cook for 1½ hours. Add salt and beans. Cook 45 minutes. Correct seasoning. The chili will have a better flavor if prepared a day in advance. Serves 16 to 18.

QUICK GANGBANG CHILI

1 cup bacon fat or shortening	6 cups tomato sauce
6 pounds ground beef	¼ cup salt
4 cups green pepper, chopped	1 teaspoon black pepper
2 cups onion, chopped	1 cup chili powder
6 Number 2½ cans tomatoes	½ cup sugar
6 Number 2 cans kidney beans	1½ cups vinegar

Melt fat in large, heavy skillet or saucepan. Add beef, green pepper and onion. Cook until meat is well browned, stirring occasionally. Add tomatoes, kidney beans, tomato sauce, salt, pepper, chili powder, sugar, vinegar. Cover and cook 25 minutes. Serves 25.

GANGBANG MEXICAN BEEF WITH OLIVES

9 pounds beef, diced	6 tablespoons tomato paste
½ cup oil	½ teaspoon Tabasco
1½ pounds ground beef	9 tablespoons chili powder
6 cloves garlic, minced	Salt and pepper
9 green peppers, quartered lengthwise	9 cups chicken broth
	6 cans corn kernels with liquid
18 onions, chopped	3 cups olives, sliced and pitted

Brown diced beef in oil with ground beef, garlic, green peppers and onions. Add tomato paste, Tabasco and chili powder, salt and pepper. Cover with chicken broth. Simmer 1½ hours. Add corn kernels with liquid. Simmer another 40 minutes until most of liquid is consumed. Add olives and heat through. If prepared early in the day, add olives just before reheating. This is good served with rice and/or tortillas. Serves 18 to 20.

GANGBANG MEXICAN CHICKEN

4 6-pound oven-ready chickens	1 teaspoon marjoram
2 teaspoons salt	6 tablespoons peanut butter
Black pepper, freshly ground	2¼ cups dry red wine
12 tablespoons oil	6 cups chicken bouillon
12 large onions, chopped	3 cups almonds, blanched
9 cloves garlic, crushed	3 cups stuffed olives, sliced
3 tablespoons sesame seeds	6 tablespoons chili powder

Season chicken with salt and pepper. Sauté in oil 15 minutes until brown on all sides. Remove and keep hot. Add onions and garlic to oil remaining in skillet. Sauté until lightly browned. Add sesame seeds, marjoram, peanut butter and wine. Simmer 5 minutes. Put chicken, onion mixture and bouillon in deep casserole. Add almonds, olives and chili powder. Cover. Bake in moderate (350°) oven 40 minutes. Uncover. Bake 15 minutes. Serves 18 to 20.

SCENE FROM *Wedding March*

GANGBANG IRISH STEW

8 pounds lamb or mutton, cut into 2- to 3-inch chunks
1¾ cups dry white wine
Salt and pepper
1 cup butter or margarine
1 cup onion, chopped
¼ cup celery, chopped
¼ cup parsley, minced
Water to cover
2 cups Irish whiskey
12 small Irish potatoes, cut in small chunks
9 small carrots, scraped and cut in thin slices
2 tablespoons Worcestershire sauce

Four hours before cooking, sprinkle meat with 1 cup wine and store in refrigerator. Turn meat several times. Remove meat. Reserve wine marinade. Sprinkle meat with salt and pepper. Brown meat in hot butter. Remove to deep heavy saucepan. Cook onion in fat until limpid. Add onion, celery, parsley and wine marinade to meat. Add water to cover. Bring to boil. Reduce heat. Cover pan. Cook over very low heat 45 minutes. Season to taste with salt and pepper. Add whiskey. Cook, covered, for 30 minutes more. Add potatoes, carrots and Worcestershire sauce. Cover. Simmer until potatoes and carrots and meat are tender. Add ¾ cup wine. Boil 5 minutes. Serve very hot. Serves 16 to 18.

BARBECUED BONED "COUNTRY STYLE" SPARERIBS

6 sides lean spareribs
1 cup soy sauce
1 cup brown sugar
3 tablespoons cornstarch
½ cup vinegar
½ cup crystallized ginger, finely chopped
3 cloves garlic, crushed

Place spareribs in roaster with 1 cup water. Cover pan and simmer until tender enough to remove bones easily — about 30 minutes. Add water occasionally to prevent browning. Cool. Remove bones. They should slip out easily. Cut meat into strips or squares. Mix soy sauce, brown sugar, cornstarch, vinegar, ginger and garlic. Dip each piece of sparerib into sauce until completely coated. Put in broiler. When top pieces are brown, turn, brush with more sauce and brown the other side. Serves 16 to 18.

These may be made in advance and reheated in the oven.

BETTY HUTTON IN *Red, Hot and Blue*

MEXICAN CHICKEN CASSEROLE

6 broiler chickens, cut up
1½ cups flour
1 tablespoon plus 1 teaspoon salt
1 teaspoon pepper
¾ cup butter
6 cups onion, chopped
2 cups green pepper, chopped

3 Number 2 cans tomatoes
3 packages frozen corn, thawed
6 cloves garlic, crushed
½ cup vinegar
½ cup chili powder
4 tablespoons peanut butter
3 teaspoons tarragon

Place flour, 1 tablespoon salt and pepper in a paper or plastic bag and shake chicken in the bag piece by piece, until each is well coated. Sauté until golden in ¼ cup butter. Turn frequently. Remove. Drain and arrange in bottom of earthenware casserole. Sauté onion and green pepper in same skillet, adding remaining butter. Add tomatoes, corn, garlic, vinegar, chili powder, peanut butter, tarragon and 1 teaspoon salt. Pour over chicken and bake, covered, in a moderately slow (325°) oven until tender — about 1 hour.

This may be made ahead, refrigerated and reheated. Rice is good with this juicy casserole.

LOVERS' LAMB STEW

1 cup oil
2¼ pounds lean leg of lamb in 2-inch pieces
2 cloves garlic, crushed
½ cup chopped onion
1 bay leaf
4 teaspoons salt
1 tablespoon celery salt
1 teaspoon basil, crushed
1 teaspoon oregano
½ teaspoon rosemary
18 small carrots, scraped

12 pearl onions, peeled
4 stalks celery, diced
1 cup flour
1 cup white wine
8 cups stock
4 tomatoes, peeled
1 Number 2 can tomato purée
4 tablespoons tomato paste
12 peppercorns
12 small potatoes, peeled
1 cup peas, fresh or frozen

Heat oil very hot in deep heavy skillet. Add pieces of lamb from which fat has been removed. Brown on all sides. Add garlic, onion, bay leaf, salt, celery salt, basil, oregano and rosemary. Add carrots, onions and celery, and sauté 5 minutes. Add flour and blend well. Mix wine, stock, tomatoes, purée, tomato paste and peppercorns. Add to skillet. Cover securely. Cook 1½ hours over slow heat. Twenty minutes before serving add potatoes. Cook 10 minutes. Add peas. Continue cooking until tender.

GANGBANG PAELLA (VALENCIA STYLE)

½ cup olive oil
2 chickens, 2½ pounds each, cut in pieces
2 medium onions, chopped
2½ cups rice
1 cup smoked ham
2 or 3 long *chorizos* (Spanish sausage) cut in ¼-inch slices
5 cloves garlic, chopped
2 teaspoons saffron

6 lobster tails, cut in half lengthwise
24 shelled shrimp
2 squids, sliced
7 cups chicken broth
4 dozen fresh clams, scrubbed
4 dozen mussels, scrubbed
24 pitted olives
6 to 8 slices pimiento
1 cup cooked green peas
2 tablespoons parsley, chopped

Sauté chicken in oil in large skillet on both sides until brown. Add onions. Simmer until slightly softened. Stir in rice, ham, *chorizos,* garlic, saffron, lobster, shrimp and squid. Add chicken broth. Cover tightly. Cook 15 to 18 minutes until rice is tender. Set aside until 20 minutes before ready to serve.

Add clams, mussels, olives and pimiento. Bake in preheated 350° oven 15 minutes. Add heated peas and parsley. Serves 16 to 20.

W. C. FIELDS IN *The Bank Dick*

DRINKS

- CAFÉ DIABLE
- CAFÉ MAZAGRAN
- CHICKADEE
  (*Gin and Curaçao*)
- SPIKED MILK
- GOODBYE, MR. CHIPS
  (*Hot Buttered Rum*)
- THE SEVENTH VEIL
  (*Bloody Mary*)
- IDIOT'S DELIGHT
  (*Black Velvet*)
- SNAKE PIT
  (*Cognac, Champagne and Stout*)
- ADAM'S RIB
  (*Vodka, Gin and Vermouth*)

- DEAD END
  (*Rye, Orange and Lemon Juice*)
- TURNABOUT
  (*Vodka and Dubonnet*)
- THE RAZOR'S EDGE
  (*Gin and Rose's Lime Juice*)
- GOLDEN BOY
  (*Bourbon and Bitters*)
- VIRGIN QUEEN
  (*Eggnog*)
- THE AWFUL TRUTH
  (*Rum, Gin and Cassis*)
- WASSAIL BEER BOWL
- CAFÉ NOVARRO
- MINT JULEP

FOOD

- BULL CUP MADRILÈNE
  (*Bourbon Madrilène*)
- OLD RUSSIAN BORSCHT
  (*Made with Vodka*)
- COQUILLES WITH JACQUES
  (*Crab Meat Coquilles*)
- SPIRAL STAIRCASE
  (*Gin and Onion Dip*)
- BOURBON BALLS

- MRS. CHENEY'S CHICKENS
  (*Chicken in Port Wine*)
- STELLA DALLAS DAUBE
  (*Beef Roast*)
- APPLES IN BOURBON
- PÂTÉ BRANDY STUFFING
- GAY DIVORCÉE
  (*Chicken Breasts*)
- CARP IN BEER

ONE man's meat is another man's poison, which is why I, myself, never drink. Well, almost never. I honestly don't mind two or three martinis for the health's sake, or perhaps a bottle of wine with dinner, to wet the whistle, as it were. But I cannot abide drunkenness. Many's the evening I found myself playing Anna Neagle (reluctantly, but once embarked upon a role I seldom abandon it) in *Nurse Edith Cavell,* succoring aid to those in need of medical attention, only to have kindness returned by ingratitude. Not even a "thank you," thank you very much. However, I must not complain. I was forewarned of the evils inherent in alcohol in *Ziegfeld Girl* with all-time favorite goddess Lana Turner, when she almost fell on her ass walking down all those stairs in that gorgeous costume. Oh, Lana, I suffered so! Lana has had her ups and downs, as we all know, but I want the world to know and you too Lana, darling, Myra's been with you all the way, through thick and thin. What began one day with *Andy Hardy,* when I first laid eyes on that gorgeous face, not to mention one of the most famous pair of breasts of all time, equal even to "those sported by Jean Harlow in *Hell's Angels* and seen at their best four minutes after the start of the second reel" (*Myra Breckinridge* — Chapter 2) has continued on to this day, *Madame X* notwithstanding. *The Lost Weekend* with wonderful Ray Milland, who was so good in *Golden Earrings* with famous grandmother sex goddess Marlene Dietrich (who, I'm proud to say, has never been divorced from her first husband and I'm even told they're still friendly, which is understandable since the word is that she's a really nice gal — and a wonderful cook) was another film that brought home to me what a drag drinking is. W. C. Fields was the only one who made the practice palatable, I suppose because he was so cute and sincere about it. He also, I might add, had a gift for it. Although even in Mr. Fields' case I cannot condone it (oh, I do hope you don't get the impression that Myra's a prude), I can appreciate anyone's actions whose motives are those of commitment. Yet, though what is sauce for the goose is not good for his gander, it probably didn't matter in Mr. Fields' case since he was not what is known in the business as a sex symbol. His appeal was on an entirely different level, not as lofty as *Imitation of Life* but valid in its own way.

Never condemning, but always compromising — the sign of intelligence and good character — cooking with alcohol not only is Myra's acceptable solution, but an enormous success as well. The reward of cooking with spirits is its own virtue. All I can do is try to persuade you to sample some of these recipes and if you don't agree with me that it's your cup of tea then Myra Breckinridge isn't all she's been cut up to be. That is a fact, Buster, and never you forget it.

DRINKS

CAFÉ DIABLE

3 cups hot black coffee
½ cup plus 2 tablespoons brandy
6 lumps sugar
4 whole cloves
Thin outer peel of 1 orange
Thin outer peel of 1 lemon
Stick of cinnamon

Heat ½ cup brandy with 5 lumps of sugar, cloves, orange and lemon peel and cinnamon in chafing dish until sugar is dissolved. Stir occasionally. Heat ladle over a match. Put remaining brandy in ladle. Add sugar lump. Light it. Lower ladle into chafing dish to light brandy mixture. While brandy is flaming, slowly pour hot coffee into chafing dish. When flames die, ladle coffee into demitasse cups.

CAFÉ MAZAGRAN

Mix double strength black coffee with equal parts of red wine. Serve very hot; sweeten to taste.

CHICKADEE
(Gin and Curaçao)

1½ ounces gin
1 ounce Lopez coconut cream
½ ounce lemon juice
½ ounce curaçao
2 ounces Seven-Up
Fresh mint

Mix all the ingredients in electric mixer with cracked ice. Serve in halved coconut with cracked ice. Garnish with fresh mint. Serves 1.

SPIKED MILK

6 teaspoons sugar	4 ounces dark rum
1 quart milk, very cold	2½ cups cracked ice
6 ounces rye whiskey	Fresh nutmeg

Put sugar in large cocktail shaker. Add half the milk. Stir until sugar is dissolved. Pour in whiskey and rum. Add ice. Shake vigorously. Divide contents of shaker, including ice, among six highball glasses. Fill with remaining milk. Sprinkle with fresh grated nutmeg. Serves 6.

GOODBYE, MR. CHIPS
(Hot Buttered Rum)

1 heaping teaspoon sugar	1 cup boiling water
6 whole cloves	3 ounces rum
1 3-inch cinnamon stick	1 tablespoon butter
Juice of ½ lemon	Pinch nutmeg
1 slice lemon	

Place sugar, cloves and cinnamon in bottom of mug. Pour lemon juice over them. Add lemon slice. Add a little hot water. Stir until sugar dissolves. Add rum and butter. Pour in boiling water. Stir until butter melts. Sprinkle with nutmeg. Serve piping hot. Serves 1.

THE SEVENTH VEIL
(Bloody Mary)

3 cups vodka	2 teaspoons catsup
3½ cups tomato juice	6 dashes Tabasco
Juice of 2 lemons	1 teaspoon salt
3 teaspoons Worcestershire	Freshly ground pepper

Pour vodka, tomato juice and lemon juice into a cold pitcher. Season with Worcestershire, catsup, Tabasco, salt and pepper. Stir well and serve very cold over ice cubes. Serves 6.

IDIOT'S DELIGHT
(Black Velvet)

1 bottle champagne, cold
4 bottles (12 ounces each) stout, cold

Chill glasses and pitcher early in the day. Pour champagne into pitcher. Add stout slowly, pouring along the side of pitcher to prevent foaming. Serve in chilled glasses.

SNAKE PIT
(Cognac, Champagne and Stout)

2 ounces Cognac
3 ounces champagne
3 ounces stout

At least one hour before mixing, chill pitcher, glasses, cognac, champagne and stout in refrigerator. Mix stout and champagne in pitcher. Pour cognac into an 8-ounce glass. Add champagne and stout. Serves 1.

ADAM'S RIB
(Vodka, Gin and Vermouth)

8 ounces vodka
8 ounces gin
3 ounces dry vermouth
6 generous pieces lemon peel

Chill 6 martini glasses. Almost fill a martini mixer with ice. Pour in vermouth. Stir well. Add gin and vodka. Stir and stir until your hand holding the mixer feels cold. Rub a piece of lemon peel around the rim of each of the chilled glasses. Drop a piece of peel into each glass and pour in drink. Serves 6.

DEAD END
(Rye, Orange and Lemon Juice)

2 ounces rye whiskey
Juice of 1 orange
Juice of 1 lemon
Crushed ice

Put whiskey in highball glass. Pour lemon and orange juices into whiskey. Fill glass with crushed ice. Stir vigorously until frost forms on outside of glass. Serve at once. Serves 1.

TURNABOUT
(Vodka and Dubonnet)

1½ cups vodka, cold
3 cups Dubonnet, cold
3 cups seltzer water, cold

Refrigerate all the ingredients, pitcher and glasses at least one hour before serving. Pour vodka into large pitcher. Add Dubonnet, then seltzer. Serve in tall glasses. Serves 6.

THE RAZOR'S EDGE
(Gin and Rose's Lime Juice)

2 ice cubes
2 ounces gin
¾ teaspoon Rose's unsweetened Lime Juice
1 slice lemon, very thin

Place cracked ice cubes in an 8-ounce glass. Pour gin over ice. Add lime juice. Fill glass with plain water. Stir well. Garnish with lemon slice. Serves 1.

GLORIA SWANSON AND WILLIAM HOLDEN IN *Sunset Boulevard*

GOLDEN BOY
(Bourbon and Bitters)

1 lump sugar	1 jigger bourbon
Dash Angostura bitters	1 crushed ice cube
Dash orange bitters	Twist lemon peel
5 dashes Pernod	

Crush sugar in 1 teaspoon water. Add remaining ingredients. Stir well. Pour into an old-fashioned glass. Rub rim of glass with lemon peel. Serves 1.

VIRGIN QUEEN
(Eggnog)

18 eggs	2 quarts bourbon
2 cups sugar	1 fifth rum
4 quarts milk	1 fifth brandy
3 quarts heavy cream	Freshly grated nutmeg

Separate eggs. Beat yolks until light. Beat in sugar gradually. Add 1 quart milk. Stir until sugar dissolves. Pour into punch bowl. Stir in cream, remaining milk, bourbon, rum and brandy. Let stand 1 hour. Fold in stiffly beaten egg white. Garnish with nutmeg. Yields about 36 drinks.

THE AWFUL TRUTH
(Rum, Gin and Cassis)

8 ounces light rum	2 ounces gin
8 ounces orange juice	2 ounces brandy
6 ounces lemon juice	4 ounces cassis syrup

Mix all ingredients in electric blender with scoop of shaved ice. Pour into bowl filled with cracked ice. Float a white carnation on top. Serve with long straws. Serves 6.

WASSAIL BEER BOWL

3 quarts hot beer
1 pound powdered sugar
1 freshly grated whole nutmeg
½ to ¾ teaspoon powdered ginger

1 cup dry sherry
4 or 5 thin slices seeded lemon
6 slices freshly made white toast

Heat beer (do not boil) with sugar, nutmeg, ginger, sherry and lemon. Bring almost to boiling point. Remove from heat. Taste for sweetening. Pour into large heated bowl containing 6 slices of freshly made toast. Serve as hot as possible in punch glasses. Serves 16 to 18.

CAFÉ NOVARRO

6 lumps sugar
Double strength coffee
Cognac

Drop lump of sugar into demitasse cup. Fill halfway with double strength coffee. Very slowly fill with cognac. Light with a match. Let it burn a few seconds. Stir. Drink it as hot as possible. Serves 6.

MINT JULEP

12 sprigs fresh mint
6 lumps sugar
6 tablespoons water
Cracked ice
12 jiggers bourbon

Crush a sprig of mint in a tall glass or goblet. Discard mint. Dissolve a lump of sugar in a tablespoon of water in each glass. Half fill each glass with cracked ice. Add 2 jiggers of bourbon. Stir gently. Garnish each with a sprig of fresh mint.

SCENE FROM *Let's Dance*

FOOD

BULL CUP MADRILÈNE
(Bourbon Madrilène)

2 pounds ground lean beef shank
2½ pounds tomatoes, chopped
Juice of ½ lemon
½ medium-sized onion, sliced
2 stalks celery, sliced
½ leek, sliced
2 medium-sized carrots, sliced
¼ cup egg whites

Freshly ground pepper
1 bay leaf
4 quarts chicken stock
9 heaping tablespoons powdered
  gelatin
Salt
1 cup bourbon
Lemon slices

Place beef, tomatoes, lemon juice, onion, celery, leek, carrots, egg whites, pepper, bay leaf and stock in a heavy kettle. Cover. Bring to a slow boil. Simmer 2 hours. Strain. Add gelatin. Season to taste. Add bourbon. Bring to a boil. Cool in refrigerator. Cut in dice. Serve with lemon slices.

OLD RUSSIAN BORSCHT
(Made with Vodka)

1½ cups jellied consommé
1½ cups cooked beets, finely
  chopped, with juice
1 cup sour cream
Salt and pepper
1 tablespoon chives, finely chopped
½ cup vodka

Blend consommé with beets, sour cream, salt and pepper to taste. Add vodka. Mix well. Serve sprinkled with chives.

COQUILLES WITH JACQUES
(Crab Meat Coquilles)

1 pound fresh or frozen lump
  crab meat
½ cup onion, minced
½ cup celery, minced
½ cup green pepper, minced
1 clove garlic, minced
1 tablespoon parsley, chopped
½ cup butter
2 cups soft bread crumbs

½ cup heavy cream
1 hard-cooked egg, chopped
1 tablespoon white wine vinegar
1 teaspoon Worcestershire
¼ teaspoon thyme
Tabasco sauce
¼ cup sherry
2 eggs, beaten
Salt

Sauté onion, celery, green pepper, garlic and parsley in ¼ cup butter 10 minutes. Cool. Add 1 cup bread crumbs, cream, chopped egg, vinegar, Worcestershire, thyme, few drops Tabasco, sherry, raw eggs and salt. Add crab meat. Toss lightly. Spoon into 12 scallop shells or individual baking dishes. Melt remaining butter and toss with remaining crumbs. Top crab mixture with buttered crumbs. Place shells in shallow baking pan. Add ¼ inch water in bottom of pan. Bake in hot (450°) oven 10 minutes until browned and hot.

SPIRAL STAIRCASE
(Gin and Onion Dip)

1 pint sour cream
1 package Lipton's dehydrated onion mix
3 ounces dry gin
2 sprigs parsley

Stir soup mix and gin into sour cream. Beat with beater (not a blender) until smooth. Garnish with parsley. Serve in a bowl surrounded with unsalted crackers or melba toast.

BOURBON BALLS

2 tablespoons Maraschino cherries
¼ cup bourbon
40 small vanilla wafers, crushed
2 tablespoons white corn syrup
2 tablespoons cocoa

¼ cup citron, cut into small pieces
⅓ cup pecans, broken into small
  pieces
Granulated sugar

Soak cherries for 12 hours in equal parts of maraschino liquid and bourbon. Mix all ingredients, except granulated sugar, thoroughly. Roll into 1¼-inch balls between the palms of the hands. If too soft, add more vanilla wafers. Roll balls in sugar. Makes 20 balls.

MRS. CHENEY'S CHICKENS
(Chicken in Port Wine)

4½ chickens, cut for fricassee	1 liqueur glass brandy
1 clove garlic, peeled	1 liqueur glass cherry brandy
½ cup light sweet port	1 cup double cream
½ cup sweet white wine	2 egg yolks

Brown chicken in butter with whole clove of garlic. Add port, wine, brandy and cherry brandy. When mixture boils, light with a match. Shake pan until flame dies. Allow sauce to simmer down to about half. Lower heat. Continue cooking until tender. Transfer chicken to serving platter and keep warm. Add double cream and egg yolks to sauce. Cook until it thickens, but do *not* boil. Stir constantly. Remove garlic. Pour over chicken and serve very hot.

STELLA DALLAS DAUBE
(Beef Roast)

4 pounds beef roast	¼ teaspoon thyme
1 large clove garlic, cut in slivers	½ cup green pepper, chopped
3 cups red wine	½ cup mushrooms
Salt and pepper	½ cup boiling water
3 tablespoons bacon grease	Marinade
¾ cup onion, sliced	Salt
1 tablespoon parsley, minced	Pepper
1 bay leaf	

Make 4 or 5 slits in roast. Insert slivers of garlic. Marinate meat in wine — covered — in refrigerator 3 to 4 hours. Turn meat several times. Remove meat. Reserve marinade. Sprinkle meat heavily with salt and pepper. Melt bacon grease in deep heavy skillet. Brown roast on all sides. Remove daube. Lightly brown onions in fat in which meat was seared. Add meat, parsley, bay leaf, thyme, green pepper, mushrooms, water and marinade. Bring to boil. Lower heat. Cover. Simmer until tender. Season gravy to taste.

APPLES IN BOURBON

6 to 8 tablespoons sugar
Rind and juice of 1 lemon
1-inch stick cinnamon

6 ounces bourbon or applejack
6 apples, peeled and cored

In top pan of chafing dish combine sugar, lemon rind and juice, cinnamon and bourbon or applejack. Place pan over low heat. Bring mixture to a boil. Add the apples (6 if apples are sweet; more, if not). Cover pan. Simmer for 35 minutes or until the apples are tender. Serve apples with sauce, hot, poured over.

PÂTÉ BRANDY STUFFING

4 slices stale bread
1 cup red wine
¼ cup dried Italian mushroom pieces
6 strips bacon
½ cup butter
1 pound chicken livers cut in small pieces
Salt and pepper

¼ cup onion, finely chopped
½ cup celery, coarsely chopped
2 tablespoons parsley, minced
¼ teaspoon basil
½ teaspoon thyme
⅛ teaspoon marjoram
⅛ teaspoon rosemary
½ cup brandy
1 egg, well beaten

Soak bread in wine 30 minutes. Soak mushrooms in water 15 minutes. Sauté bacon. Remove bread and squeeze. Set aside ½ cup wine squeezed from bread. Melt 2 tablespoons butter until it bubbles (360°). Sprinkle livers with salt and pepper. Sauté livers 5 minutes in butter and bacon fat. Add onion, celery, parsley and drained mushrooms. Cook until onion is clear. Mash half the livers while cooking. Reduce heat. Add bread, ¼ cup wine (reserved from bread), basil, thyme, marjoram, rosemary and crumbled bacon. Cook, stirring and mashing until there are no lumps. When bread begins to brown, stir in brandy and continue cooking over low heat, stirring constantly, until well blended. Remove from heat. Cool. Blend in remaining softened butter and egg. Season with salt and pepper. If not perfectly smooth, pass through food grinder.

This is good for turkey and chicken. It makes about 2½ quarts stuffing. If you omit bread and egg, it's a divine pâté spread.

DOROTHY LAMOUR, HENRY FONDA,
GEORGE RAFT AND JOHN BARRYMORE IN *Spawn of the North*

GAY DIVORCÉE
(Chicken Breasts)

1 cup dry sherry
6 fryer double breasts, boned
Salt and pepper
½ cup butter
6 thick slices ham

½ cup Napoleon brandy
1 cup whole canned or fresh sliced
    mushrooms
1½ cups whipping cream

Marinate chicken breasts in sherry in refrigerator for 3 to 4 hours. Turn 2 or 3 times. Remove. Sprinkle breasts with salt and pepper. Heat butter until bubbly. Add chicken. Brown on both sides. Just before removing from skillet, sprinkle 2 tablespoons sherry marinade over each. Pin a thick slice of ham around each breast. Brush with brandy. Place in baking dish. Add mushrooms and cream. Cover baking dish with aluminum foil. Bake 1 hour in 350° oven.

CARP IN BEER

4-pound carp, cleaned
1 tablespoon salt
3 cups dark or light beer
2 onions, finely chopped
1 bay leaf

6 whole peppercorns
1 lemon, sliced
1 tablespoon butter
1 tablespoon flour
1 tablespoon sugar

Cut carp into serving pieces. Sprinkle with salt. Set aside for 30 minutes. Place fish in stew pan with beer, onions, bay leaf, peppercorns and lemon. Put pan over medium heat. Simmer gently 15 to 20 minutes, until fish is tender. Remove fish to heated platter. Blend butter with flour. Stir in broth and sugar. Continue to cook for a few minutes. Stir constantly. Strain sauce and pour over fish.

MIKE YELLEN AND JERRY LEWIS IN *At War with the Army*

- BUTTERMILK SOUP
- GUMBO DELIGHT
- CARROT SOUP
- CHICKEN SHERRY CREAM
- BLACK SPAGHETTI
- VEAL AND BEET BORSCHT
- ARTICHOKE AND CRAB MEAT SALAD
- MAE WEST CHICKEN SALAD
- SPANISH CUCUMBER SALAD
- SPANISH TUNA AND OLIVES
- TUNA AND WHITE BEAN SALAD
- NEW ENGLAND CLAM PIE
- BAKED CODFISH NEW ORLEANS
- SHRIMP AND OYSTER JAMBALAYA
- FLOUNDER AND CAVIAR
- BAKED LAMB CHOPS IN RED WINE
- STUFFED VEAL BIRDS
- VEAL GOULASH
- VEAL WITH TENDER PEAS
- TONGUE AND SPINACH BRULÉE
- FRANKFURTER AND ONION CASSEROLE

- HERBAL FRIED ONIONS
- EGGPLANT PROVENÇALE
- RATATOUILLE
- FENNEL STUFFED WITH DILL BUTTER
- ENDIVES AU GRATIN
- POMMES DE TERRE À LA CRÈME
- CHOUCROUTE AU CHAMPAGNE
- SWEET-SOUR RED CABBAGE
- GNOCCHI À LA PARISIENNE
- PEACHES WITH WINE
- BANANAS AU RHUM FLAMBÉ
- WEST INDIAN BOILED BANANAS
- BAKED BANANAS
- RUM OMELETTE
- COURT BOUILLON
- BROWN SAUCE
- SAUCE BIGARADE
- FRENCH DRESSING
- MAYONNAISE
- TOMATO SAUCE
- UNRECTIFIABLE SCREW-UPS

EVEN if you follow this book to the letter, you're bound to screw-up, everybody does. Nobody's perfect. We are all entitled to our little mistakes. That is why I have included this chapter for novices and veterans alike. You will find that no amount of planning, shopping or preparation will make you immune to an occasional lapse of talent in the kitchen. The butter burns and the shops are closed. Your soufflé just won't rise no matter what you do to it. The syrup is salty instead of sweet. What does one do at moments like this? Your guest is waiting — you just can't let him sit there dangling. This chapter will solve all your problems. Substitute dishes for the grand ones you'd had in mind, but just as good nevertheless, a choice of recipes that you can whip up in a matter of minutes, and last but not least the names and telephone numbers of some very important suppliers. So just relax, honey. (I myself hate to be called "honey," resembling in this the former First Lady — *Myra Breckinridge*, Chapter 21.) Fix your makeup. Try that new brassière or none. And *enter* like Loretta Young (a true goddess of the silver screen *and* the television world) and in a voice reminiscent of the late Ann Sheridan in *Doughgirls*, sweetly and huskily drop the news that "this one will be a quickie." You'll still find your way to his heart. But don't stop there, because if that's all you've learned from this book, then you might just as well order up a Danish pastry and coffee.

TONY CURTIS AND MARILYN MONROE ON THE SET OF *Some Like it Hot*

BUTTERMILK SOUP

6 walnuts, shelled
Dash of salt
2 cloves garlic, crushed
½ cup olive oil
2 tablespoons water

2 tablespoons vinegar
1½ quarts buttermilk
2 cucumbers, chopped
Salt
Pepper

Mash nuts with salt. Add garlic and oil. Mash to a thick paste. Blend in water and vinegar. Stir mixture into buttermilk. Add cucumber. Season with salt and pepper. Serve cold. Serves 4.

GUMBO DELIGHT

4 cups bouillon
1 clove garlic, crushed
1 tablespoon Worcestershire
1 tablespoon gumbo filé

12 black olives, pitted
½ cup dry sherry
2 tablespoons parsley, chopped

Put bouillon, garlic and Worcestershire in a large saucepan. Sprinkle with gumbo filé. Cook over low heat. Slice olives lengthwise. Add to soup. Just before serving, bring soup to boil — stir in sherry. Pour into soup cups. Garnish with chopped parsley. Serves 2 or 3.

CARROT SOUP

2½ cups carrots, sliced
½ teaspoon salt
1¾ cups water
1 can (13 ounces) undiluted cream
of chicken soup

¼ teaspoon each coarse ground pepper and fresh ground nutmeg
1 tablespoon parsley, minced

Cook carrots in salted water until tender. Blend carrots and water in which they were cooked in an electric blender until smooth. Return to saucepan. Add chicken soup, pepper, nutmeg and parsley. Return to heat. Bring to a boil.

CHICKEN SHERRY CREAM

1 10½-ounce can cream of chicken
soup
1 cup cooked chicken, cut into cubes
1 13-ounce can madrilène

½ cup whipping cream
¾ cup sherry
Chopped chives

Blend chicken soup and chicken in electric blender. Bring madrilène to a boil. Pour into chicken mixture. Blend slowly until mixed. Add cream and sherry. Blend thoroughly. Serve in cups sprinkled with chives.

BLACK SPAGHETTI

1 pound spaghetti
4 quarts boiling salted water
3 tablespoons olive or salad oil
2 medium onions, finely chopped
2 cloves garlic, minced
1 or 2 jars pitted black olives

4 slices bacon, cut into bits
5 anchovy fillets, chopped, or 2 to 3
teaspoons anchovy paste
3 tablespoons parsley, chopped
4 tablespoons cheese, grated

Boil spaghetti until *al dente* (firm, not too soft). Sauté onions in two tablespoons oil. Add garlic, olives, bacon, anchovies or anchovy paste and parsley. Cook until bacon is crisp. Place drained spaghetti in serving dish with remaining oil. Mix well. Cover with sauce. Serve with grated cheese. Serves 4.

NOTE: You'll find other quick pasta substitutes in Chapter 5 — Good Enough to Eat.

VEAL AND BEET BORSCHT

2 ounces lean veal cut in small pieces
2 ounces beets, cooked
1 cucumber, peeled and thinly sliced
2 cups sour cream
1 teaspoon powdered dill
1 teaspoon salt

½ teaspoon pepper
1 teaspoon chives, cut in very small
pieces
12 large shrimps
6 hard-boiled eggs, peeled and sliced

Cook veal in salted water to cover until tender. Purée beets in a

ELSA LANCHESTER IN *Bride of Frankenstein*

blender, or pass through a sieve, with their water. Add cucumber to beets and beet water. Mix into veal and its juices. Gradually stir in sour cream. Add dill, salt, pepper, chives and shrimps. Garnish with eggs. Serve ice cold.

If there is no time to chill in the refrigerator set in freezer 10 to 15 minutes.

ARTICHOKE AND CRAB MEAT SALAD

1 cup diced cooked artichoke hearts	½ cup catsup
1 cup crab meat chunks	½ teaspoon Worcestershire
½ cup heavy cream, whipped	1 or 2 drops Tabasco
1 cup mayonnaise	Salt and pepper to taste

Combine artichokes and crab meat. Chill in refrigerator. Mix whipped cream with mayonnaise, catsup, Worcestershire, Tabasco, salt and pepper. Chill in refrigerator. Serve crab meat and artichokes topped with sauce.

If time is short, place in freezer compartment 10 minutes.

MAE WEST CHICKEN SALAD

2 cups cooked chicken, thinly sliced	¼ teaspoon salt
1 can water chestnuts, thinly sliced	Black pepper to taste, freshly ground
2 cups seedless green grapes	1 teaspoon soy sauce
1 cup mayonnaise	1 cup honeydew balls
½ teaspoon curry powder	1 cup cantaloupe balls
1 tablespoon lemon juice	

Combine chicken, water chestnuts and grapes. Mix mayonnaise with curry powder, lemon juice, salt, pepper and soy sauce. Mix chicken with dressing. Add honeydew and cantaloupe balls. Toss all together.

EDDIE CANTOR IN *Palmy Days*

SPANISH CUCUMBER SALAD

2 Spanish onions, thinly sliced
2 cucumbers, peeled and thinly sliced
5 ripe tomatoes, thinly sliced
2 tablespoons dry bread crumbs

2 tablespoons vinegar
5 tablespoons olive oil
1 small clove garlic, crushed
Salt and pepper

Alternate layers of onions, cucumbers, tomatoes, bread crumbs, salt, pepper, ending with tomatoes, topped with bread crumbs. Pour over French dressing made with olive oil, vinegar, garlic clove, salt and pepper. Chill thoroughly in refrigerator — or quick chill in the freezer 10 to 15 minutes.

SPANISH TUNA AND OLIVES

1 can tuna
1 can or jar green or black olives
¾ tablespoon butter or margarine
¾ tablespoon flour
½ cup sherry or white wine

2 teaspoons lemon juice
Pepper to taste
½ teaspoon lemon rind
1 tablespoon parsley, chopped

Melt butter in saucepan. Blend in flour. Add sherry, lemon juice and pepper. Cook, stirring constantly until thick and smooth. Add tuna, lemon rind and olives. Heat thoroughly. Garnish with parsley. Serves 2 or 3.

TUNA AND WHITE BEAN SALAD

1 cup tuna fish chunks, drained
2 cans white beans
1 red onion, cut in paper-thin slices
½ cup olive oil

1 teaspoon salt
1 teaspoon basil
2 tablespoons wine vinegar
Fresh ground black pepper

Combine all ingredients. Toss well. Refrigerate for several hours before serving.

NEW ENGLAND CLAM PIE

3 cans minced clams
½ pound bacon, diced
2 onions, chopped
2 carrots, chopped
1 bay leaf
3 potatoes, diced
1 clove garlic, crushed

½ teaspoon pepper
Pinch nutmeg
Salt
2 tablespoons flour
2 tablespoons butter
½ package pastry mix for top crust,
    prepared as directed on package

Drain clams. Reserve liquor. Chop coarsely. Fry bacon. Remove from pan. Set aside. Sauté onions and carrots in bacon drippings for a few minutes. Add ½ cup water, bay leaf and potatoes. Simmer a few minutes. Add clam liquor: about 2 to 2½ cups. Cook until vegetables are tender. Remove bay leaf. Add clams, crumbled bacon, garlic, pepper, nutmeg and a little salt to taste. Dissolve flour in 2 tablespoons water. Stir into mixture. Cook until thickened. Pour into a casserole. Dot with butter. Cover with prepared pie crust. Make a few slashes in top to let steam escape. Bake in 450° oven 20 minutes.

BAKED CODFISH NEW ORLEANS

4-pound codfish
Lemon juice
1 cup dry bread crumbs
4 tablespoons melted butter
1 tablespoon parsley, finely chopped
1 teaspoon chives, minced
2 tablespoons onion, grated
Juice and grated rind of 1 lemon
2 tablespoons ham, finely chopped

¼ teaspoon thyme
Dash nutmeg
Salt and pepper
2 cups stewed tomatoes
1 teaspoon parsley, finely chopped
½ cup raw mushrooms, sliced
½ tablespoon flour
1½ tablespoons butter

Rub inside of codfish with lemon juice. Prepare stuffing: Blend bread crumbs, melted butter, parsley, chives, onion, juice and rind of lemon with ham, thyme, nutmeg, salt and pepper to taste. Stuff cavity of codfish. Skewer closed.

Place fish in well-buttered baking dish. Add tomatoes, parsley and mushrooms. Bake covered in hot oven 20 minutes. Remove fish and keep warm. Stir flour and butter into sauce. Return fish to baking dish. Cover. Bake in moderate oven 20 minutes longer.

SHRIMP AND OYSTER JAMBALAYA

2 cups rice
½ cup oil
3 onions, chopped
2 bell peppers, chopped
4 stalks celery, chopped
2 cloves garlic, crushed
1 ham bone
2 cups cooked or canned tomatoes
2 teaspoons salt

Fresh ground pepper
2 teaspoons sugar
Bay leaf, crushed
⅛ teaspoon thyme
2 tablespoons parsley, chopped
2½ cups boiling water
3 cups cooked shrimp
2 dozen oysters

Brown rice lightly in oil. Remove and set aside. Add onions, peppers, celery, garlic and ham bone to oil. Sauté a few minutes. Add tomatoes, salt, pepper, sugar, bay leaf, thyme and parsley. Simmer 5 minutes. Mix in rice, boiling water, shrimp and oysters. Cover. Simmer slowly about 20 minutes until rice is tender. Remove ham bone. Cut away any meat on ham bone and dice. Mix into jambalaya before serving. Serves 6.

FLOUNDER AND CAVIAR

3 pounds fresh or frozen flounder fillets
3 cups dry white wine
Juice of 2 lemons
2 teaspoons salt
¼ teaspoon white pepper
3 tablespoons flour

3 tablespoons butter
1 cup scalded half-and-half (half milk and half cream)
1 egg yolk, well beaten
Salt and white pepper
3 tablespoons red or black caviar

Poach flounder in white wine with lemon juice, 2 tablespoons salt and ¼ teaspoon pepper. When flesh flakes easily, lift fish to hot platter. Set aside in warm oven. Stir flour into melted butter. Stir constantly. Do not allow to brown. Add 1 cup fish stock and the half-and-half. Cook, stirring continuously until sauce thickens. Add a small amount of sauce to egg yolk. Blend well. Stir yolk into sauce. Season with salt and pepper. Serve fish topped with sauce and garnished with caviar. Serve at once.

TONY CURTIS AND JACK LEMMON IN *Some Like it Hot*

BAKED LAMB CHOPS IN RED WINE

6 shoulder lamb chops	1 onion, chopped
Garlic	2 tablespoons shallots, chopped
Salt	1 tablespoon parsley, chopped
Black pepper	1½ tablespoons flour
4 tablespoons butter	1½ cups dry red wine

Rub chops with garlic, salt and pepper. Brown chops on both sides in 2 tablespoons butter. Transfer to baking dish. Keep them hot. Meanwhile, sauté onion, shallots and parsley in 2 tablespoons butter. When soft, blend in flour. Add wine gradually. Cook until sauce thickens. Stir constantly. Pour sauce over lamb chops. Cover casserole with buttered paper. Bake in moderate oven 20 minutes until chops are tender. Remove paper and cook 10 minutes longer.

STUFFED VEAL BIRDS

1½ pounds veal scallopine, pounded thin	Salt and pepper
1 large onion, finely chopped	4 tablespoons sherry
3 tablespoons butter	1 teaspoon tomato paste
2 hard-boiled eggs, shelled and chopped	2 teaspoons potato flour
2 tablespoons mixed parsley, sage and oregano	1 cup stock
	1 bay leaf
	4 cups cooked rice

Cook onion in butter until soft. Add eggs, herbs, salt and pepper. Spread on each veal slice. Roll carefully. Fasten at each end with toothpick. Brown quickly in butter. Stir in 3 tablespoons sherry. Heat through. Remove birds from pan. Stir tomato paste and potato flour into the pan. Stir until smooth. Add stock. Season. Stir until mixture comes to a boil. Add bay leaf, and 1 tablespoon sherry. Return veal birds to pan. Cover. Cook slowly 20 minutes. Remove bay leaf. Serve with buttered rice.

BING CROSBY IN *High Time*

VEAL GOULASH

4 cups diced leftover veal
2 cups onion, thinly sliced
½ cup butter
1 tablespoon sweet paprika
1 tablespoon hot paprika
½ teaspoon thyme

1 teaspoon caraway seeds
2 cups beef bouillon
½ cup dry white wine
3 tablespoons flour
Hot buttered noodles

Sauté onion in ¼ cup butter 5 minutes. Brown meat in remaining butter. Add paprikas, thyme, onion and caraway. Cook 10 minutes. Stir frequently. Mix bouillon and wine with flour. Add slowly to veal mixture. Cook, stirring constantly, until thickened. Serve over noodles.

VEAL WITH TENDER PEAS

4 pounds lean veal cutlet, cut in
    1-inch cubes
5 celery stalks with leaves
4 sprigs parsley
1 bay leaf
1½ tablespoons thyme
8 whole cloves

Salt
Pepper
3 tablespoons butter
3 tablespoons flour
6 tablespoons sherry
Cayenne
3 cups cooked peas

Put veal cubes in water to cover with celery, parsley, bay leaf, thyme, cloves, salt and pepper. Simmer until veal is tender — about 20 minutes. Remove veal. Strain broth. Set aside. Brown veal in butter over high heat. Stir well. Reduce heat. Add flour. Mix well into meat and butter. Remove from heat. Gradually stir in 2 cups of veal broth. Cook, stirring constantly about 15 minutes. Stir in sherry and a few pinches cayenne. Add peas. Heat a few minutes and serve.

TONGUE AND SPINACH BRULÉE

1 (1 pound 3 ounce) jar smoked
    tongue
2 packages frozen spinach
6 tablespoons flour
6 tablespoons butter

3 cups milk
½ teaspoon salt
¼ teaspoon pepper
Cheddar cheese, grated

Cut tongue into 8 to 12 slices. Cook spinach according to package directions. Make cream sauce by blending flour into melted butter. Add milk. Cook until thick, stirring constantly. Season with salt and pepper. Drain spinach. Arrange in bottom of shallow casserole. Lay tongue slices on spinach. Pour sauce over tongue. Sprinkle generously with grated cheese. Place under low broiler 10 minutes to heat tongue and brown top. Serves 4.

FRANKFURTER AND ONION CASSEROLE

12 frankfurters	⅛ teaspoon thyme
2 cloves garlic, cut in half	⅛ teaspoon mace
Bacon drippings	Pinch nutmeg
2 large onions, thinly sliced	1 small bay leaf
Fresh mushrooms	1 large green pepper, thinly sliced
Salt and pepper	1 cup tomato purée

Rub bottom of an earthenware casserole with garlic cloves; then grease well with bacon drippings. Lay frankfurters in casserole. Top with onions. Cover with mushrooms. Season to taste with salt, pepper, thyme, mace, nutmeg, bay leaf and green pepper. Pour in the tomato purée. Cover tightly. Bake in hot (400°) oven 30 minutes.

HERBAL FRIED ONIONS

2 tablespoons butter (or 1 tablespoon each butter and olive oil)
4 medium-large onions
Salt and pepper
⅔ teaspoon sweet marjoram
Dash cayenne

In an iron skillet melt butter or butter and olive oil. When fat is hot but not smoking, throw in onions. Salt and pepper them. Add marjoram and cayenne. Stir until onions are all covered with oil. Cover. Cook over fairly slow heat 10 to 15 minutes until onions are wilted, slightly golden and tender but not mushy. Add more salt if needed. If surplus moisture has collected, cook, uncovered, over higher heat.

MICKEY ROONEY IN *Babes on Broadway*

EGGPLANT PROVENÇALE

6 small eggplants
Salt and pepper
6 tablespoons olive oil
3 tomatoes, peeled and coarsely chopped

1 clove garlic, crushed
2 anchovies, diced
1 tablespoon basil, chopped
6 lemon slices
6 black olives, pitted

Cut unpeeled eggplants in 1½-inch-thick slices. Season with salt and pepper. Brown lightly on all sides in hot olive oil. Remove from heat. Drain on absorbent paper. To the same oil add tomatoes, salt, pepper, garlic and anchovies. Heat slowly until tomatoes are cooked. Remove from heat. Add basil. Place 1 teaspoon of sauce on each slice of eggplant. Garnish with lemon slices, more anchovy and black olives.

RATATOUILLE

Scant ¼ cup olive oil
3 cloves garlic, crushed
4 large onions, thinly sliced
4 green peppers, seeded and quartered
1 medium-sized eggplant, sliced ¼-inch thick

6 small zucchini, sliced ¼-inch thick
6 medium-sized tomatoes, thinly sliced
Salt and pepper

Heat olive oil in bottom of casserole with garlic. Add in layers: onions, green peppers, eggplant, zucchini and tomatoes. Salt and pepper each layer lightly. Add a few drops of olive oil on the surface. Cook the ratatouille over high heat 30 minutes, gently stirring occasionally. Cook uncovered the last 10 minutes. Good hot or cold.

FENNEL STUFFED WITH DILL BUTTER

¾ pound soft cream cheese
¾ pound sweet butter
2 tablespoons heavy sweet cream
3 tablespoons cognac
5 tablespoons fresh dill, minced
About 40 fennel stalks — 6 or 7 fennel

Mix cream cheese, butter and sweet cream with cognac and dill. Fill each fennel stalk with this mixture, or squeeze through a pastry bag into the centers of fennel stalks. Chill well before serving.

ENDIVES AU GRATIN

2 pearl onions, chopped
3 tablespoons melted butter
1 pound mushrooms, finely ground
Salt and pepper to taste
3 cans endives

1 cup Béchamel Sauce (see page 137)
2 tablespoons Swiss cheese, grated
3 tablespoons Parmesan cheese, grated

Brown onions in 1 tablespoon melted butter. Add mushrooms. Cook until liquid evaporates. Add salt and pepper. Brown endives in remaining 2 tablespoons of melted butter. Lay mushrooms and onions in baking dish. Top with endives. Cover with Béchamel Sauce. Sprinkle with cheese. Brown in hot (450°) oven.

POMMES DE TERRE À LA CRÈME

8 medium-sized potatoes
2 cups milk
¼ teaspoon salt
A little white pepper

Dash nutmeg
2 tablespoons butter
3 tablespoons heavy cream
Parsley, chopped

Boil potatoes in their skins in salted water until tender. Drain. Peel. Cut in ¼-inch slices. Put slices in saucepan with just enough hot milk to cover. Add salt, pepper and nutmeg. Bring to a boil. Cook until milk is reduced to about half original quantity. Add butter and cream. Fold carefully — do not break potatoes. Correct seasoning. Serve garnished with parsley.

CHOUCROUTE AU CHAMPAGNE

2 pounds sauerkraut
2 to 3 cups champagne
3 slices fresh pineapple, 1 inch thick, cut into pieces

Drain sauerkraut. Place in saucepan with champagne to cover. Simmer sauerkraut very slowly until tender. Add pineapple for 5 minutes. Serve garnished with pineapple chunks.

SWEET-SOUR RED CABBAGE

1 large onion, chopped
4 tablespoons butter
1 head red cabbage, chopped
1 teaspoon salt
¼ teaspoon pepper

1 tablespoon flour
½ cup vinegar
2 tablespoons sugar
1 teaspoon caraway seeds

Sauté onion in butter until light brown. Add cabbage, ½ cup water, salt and pepper. Simmer covered 15 minutes. Mix flour, vinegar, sugar and caraway seeds. Stir into cabbage. Cook uncovered 5 minutes.

GNOCCHI À LA PARISIENNE

¼ pound pot cheese
2 packages cream cheese
Salt
Cayenne pepper
Pinch chili pepper

1 tablespoon sour cream
¾ cup cake flour
4 quarts boiling salted water
Butter
Paprika

Mix pot cheese and cream cheese with salt, cayenne pepper, chili pepper and sour cream. Mix carefully with flour. Roll into a long rope on a floured board. Cut in pieces ¾ inch thick. Drop one at a time into slowly boiling water. Lower heat. Poach 15 minutes until firm. Drain well. Sprinkle with paprika. Bake in moderate oven 15 minutes. Serve with melted butter.

PEACHES WITH WINE

6 firm, ripe peaches, peeled
2 cups dry white wine
1 cup cold water
1 tablespoon lemon juice
2 strips lemon peel, 2 inches long
¾ to 1 cup sugar

Combine wine, water, lemon juice, lemon peel and sugar. Simmer until sugar dissolves. Add peaches to syrup. Bring to a boil. Lower heat. Simmer until peaches are tender. Chill.

BANANAS AU RHUM FLAMBÉ

2 tablespoons butter
Bananas, peeled and sliced in half
   lengthwise

Brown sugar
Cinnamon
2 ounces warm rum

Place bananas in melted butter in top of chafing dish, directly over flame. Sprinkle with sugar and cinnamon. Sauté until lightly browned on both sides. When soft *but not mushy,* add heated rum and ignite.

WEST INDIAN BOILED BANANAS

6 green-tipped or underripe yellow
   bananas, peeled
1 cup dry white wine
Dash of salt

1 heaping tablespoon butter
2 tablespoons flour
Pinch each nutmeg, cinnamon, cloves,
   cayenne

Cut bananas in half. Put in saucepan with wine and salt. Bring to a boil. Cover. Simmer over low heat 20 minutes. Blend butter and flour together. Season with nutmeg, cinnamon, cloves and cayenne. Add a little at a time to banana mixture. Cook 2 to 3 minutes. Serve hot.

BAKED BANANAS

6 bananas, peeled and cut lengthwise
⅓ cup white corn syrup
3 tablespoons lemon juice

3 tablespoons orange juice
3 tablespoons Cointreau

Put bananas into buttered shallow baking dish. Mix corn syrup with fruit juices. Pour over bananas. Bake in moderate (350°) oven 15 to 20 minutes. Sprinkle with Cointreau just before serving.

RUM OMELETTE

6 eggs mixed with 4 tablespoons cold
   water
1½ tablespoons butter

Salt
Sugar
½ cup rum, heated

Beat eggs and water until just blended. Melt butter in top pan of a chafing dish over direct flame. Add egg mixture. Cook over medium flame. Stir sides with a wooden fork. Tilt pan so that uncooked egg

WILLIAM POWELL

runs around rim of pan. Sprinkle omelette lightly with salt. Turn carefully. When set, fold in half and top with sugar. Pour in rum. Set on fire. While rum is burning, dip up some of it and ladle it over omelette.

COURT BOUILLON (1 quart)

Fish heads, bones and skin	12 black peppercorns
3 cups water	½ onion, sliced
1 cup white wine	1 sprig parsley
½ cup white vinegar	1 small carrot, sliced
1 bay leaf	1 tablespoon salt

Boil all ingredients 20 minutes.

BROWN SAUCE (1 cup)

1 heaping tablespoon butter	1 tablespoon tomato purée
½ heaping tablespoon flour	Salt
1 cup consommé or any stock	Pepper

Brown flour in melted butter until light brown. Add hot stock. Stir again to dissolve lumps. Add tomato purée, and salt and pepper to taste. Simmer slowly 10 minutes. Strain. Add meat drippings if available. (Remember to stir flour constantly until brown.)

SAUCE BIGARADE (2 cups)

1 cup port	⅛ teaspoon coriander
1 orange, medium, juice and peel cut into matchstick lengths	3 cups meat or poultry drippings
4 tablespoons currant jelly	Salt
1 medium bay leaf	2 tablespoons cornstarch

Heat port, orange peel and juice in skillet. Reduce to half. Add jelly, bay leaf, coriander, and drippings. Reduce again. Remove bay leaf. Salt to taste. Dissolve cornstarch in two tablespoons port wine. Stir into sauce to thicken.

FRENCH DRESSING (1 cup)

¾ cup olive oil (or ½ salad oil, ½ olive oil)
¼ cup lemon juice (or vinegar, or half and half)
1 teaspoon salt
¼ teaspoon pepper

Blend lemon juice (or vinegar) well with salt and pepper. Stir in oil. Mix until well blended.

VARIATIONS

• Add 1 crushed garlic clove — or rub the salad bowl with garlic
• Add 1 teaspoon grated onion and a pinch of sugar
• Add 1 tablespoon finely chopped chives
• Add 3 tablespoons crushed or crumbled Roquefort cheese
• Mix in 1 tablespoon prepared mustard
• Add ¼ cup raw mushrooms, thinly sliced
• Use tarragon vinegar

MAYONNAISE (1 cup)

2 egg yolks
1 cup olive oil
½ teaspoon dry mustard
½ teaspoon salt
2 tablespoons lemon juice

Mix egg yolks in a warm bowl with mustard and salt. Beat with a rotary beater until well blended. Add ¼ cup olive oil, drop by drop, beating continually until thick and smooth. Repeat until all the oil has been well blended into the yolk mixture. Then add, very slowly, the lemon juice. The mayonnaise should be thick and glossy. If the mayonnaise should curdle, beat 1 egg cold in another bowl and slowly add — with a clean beater — the curdled mayonnaise.

All this may be done in an electric blender at medium mixing speed, or with an electric egg beater.

TOMATO SAUCE (1 quart)

3 tablespoons olive oil
1 cup onion, finely chopped
¼ cup celery, minced
2 cloves garlic, minced
1 (1 pound) can Italian peeled to-
    matoes
2 tablespoons tomato paste
1 teaspoon oregano
1 teaspoon salt
1 teaspoon sugar
Fresh ground black pepper to taste

Sauté onions, celery and garlic in olive oil until onions are transparent — not brown. Add the remaining ingredients. Cook covered over low heat for about an hour. Taste and correct seasoning.

UNRECTIFIABLE SCREW-UPS

LAUREL AND HARDY

Name	Address	Telephone
Pizza		
Chinese Food		
Delicatessen		
Chicken Dee-Lite		
Hamburgers		

RESTAURANTS — RESERVATIONS

INDEX